Reading Aids Series

Charles T. Mangrum, *Series Editor*
University of Miami

Reading Tests for the Secondary Grades: A Review and Evaluation

William Blanton, Roger Farr, and J. Jaap Tuinman
Editors
Indiana University

An IRA Service Bulletin

Published by the
INTERNATIONAL READING ASSOCIATION • Newark, Delaware

Library of Congress Catalog Card Number: 70-190453
Second Printing, October 1972

CONTENTS

This Reading Aid was developed under the auspices of the members of the IRA Evaluation of Tests Committee:

William Blanton
Frederick B. Davis
Roger Farr
Walter Hill
Marjorie Seddon Johnson
Lawrence M. Kasdon
Carolyn E. Massad
Nancy Roser
Robert Schreiner
J. Jaap Tuinman

FOREWORD

The need for classes in developmental reading at the secondary school level was recognized before World War II, and a few schools pioneered in offering such courses. In the decades that followed, secondary schools increasingly saw the need and provided some students, at least, with the opportunity to acquire reading skills commensurate with their levels of ability, achievement, and purposes. A few schools instituted reading courses for all their students, and some forward looking state departments of education required a course in the teaching of reading for initial certification of all secondary school teachers.

If the secondary school accepts the obligation of teaching all students to read at the level of their abilities, then the materials and methods employed need to be appropriate to the levels of the learners. How to determine these levels is a continual problem, for the longer the students stay in school, the greater the range of achievement becomes within a given class and the greater the opportunity for variation in the specific skills each student possesses.

The Reading Aids Series was designed to provide practical suggestions, and this one presents ideas for utilizing standardized tests along with an informal inventory to determine the reading levels of secondary school students. It also includes comprehensive reviews of the most commonly used standardized tests for high school students and gives information about their construction, standardization, administration, and use. Furthermore, the booklet serves as a kind of sequel to another IRA publication, *Tests of Readiness: A Review and Evaluation* by Roger Farr and Nicholas Anastasiow, 1971.

Teachers in the secondary school, whether specifically assigned to teach classes in reading or in other subjects, should find this collection helpful and practical, for it brings together data that would be difficult and time-consuming to assemble. The authors have completed a task that ought to facilitate reading improvement for the pupils. The International Reading Association takes pleasure in presenting this newest Reading Aid to its members and others interested in reading instruction.

Helen Huus, *President*
International Reading Association
1969-1970

Chapter 1

CRITERIA FOR REVIEWING TESTS*

• Why Such A Book As This One?

This book is intended primarily for classroom teachers and other personnel who are directly concerned with selecting reading achievement tests. One may ask, "Does one really need a guide to select a test?" All readers have probably had a course in tests and measurements and know the general rules for selecting an achievement test. Many, however, had the course before actually teaching so that theory was too removed from practice and, therefore, was not so useful as it could have been. But, more importantly, test development has made rapid advancement in theory and practice in recent years.

Selecting a reading achievement test is continually becoming a more complex task with these advancements. Test manufacturing has become a large scale enterprise with attractive and highly promoted reading achievement, assessment, and diagnostic devices. Some of these instruments are based on new research evidence on how children learn to read. Other tests are designed specifically to measure experimental programs, rather than the more traditional approaches.

The computer has also made an impact on test construction. Rapid analyses of the statistical characteristics of a test are now possible. In the past it would have taken months or years to analyze the results of each item on a test given to a large sample of children. Using rapid analysis techniques, the computer has enabled test manufacturers to revise their tests more frequently, and the revision of old tests is based on more accurate and complete information about the effectiveness of each test question.

Old tests, however, remain in the schools long after the curriculum has been changed. These tests are outdated and no longer serve the purpose for which they were originally designed. Yet, on the other hand, some of the older tests still are the "best" that are currently available. How does a teacher choose among them? Selecting a test takes time and careful evaluation, more time than the classroom teacher has to give from his other instructional duties. This monograph is designed to review the major issues that should be considered before a test is chosen and used in a classroom.

The authors have reviewed several of the most commonly used reading achievement tests currently available for use with high school students and have evaluated these instruments as to both their content and statistical characteristics. An analysis of the research reports from the ERIC Clearing-

*This chapter is a reprint, with minor adaptations, from R. Farr and N. Anastasiow, *Tests of Reading Readiness and Achievement: A Review and Evaluation,* International Reading Association, Newark, Delaware, 1971.

house on Retrieval of Information and Evaluation on Reading was consulted in an attempt to determine which reading tests were being used most often.

These test reviews will hopefully serve as a guide for evaluation in selecting the appropriate test for use in a specific classroom. This guide should reduce the time normally spent in evaluating reading tests. The issues considered by the reviewers in evaluating the tests are the content measured by the test, its statistical properties, its scorability, the meaning of the subtest and total test scores, and whether the test measures adequately what it purports to measure. Although the results are summarized, it may be useful to review the purposes and uses of achievement tests.

• Why Use a Commercially Prepared Reading Achievement Test?

Prediction and Assessment

One's observation of a student's daily performance is the main source for determining how well a student is doing. One will also, however, want to make periodic controlled assessment of each student's current reading ability in order to place him at his appropriate instructional level. Teachers are aware that a student makes the most rapid progress when instruction is near his current level of mastery. Thus, tests help teachers make initial, rough assessments so that instruction can begin with a better probability of success.

Teacher-made tests are one of the main sources of gathering data about children in a classroom. These results help one to predict future achievement, assess how well children have accomplished the goals, and provide feedback to the child as well as reinforce the student for what he has accomplished. However useful these results may be, teachers, parents, and administrators are prone to want some outside assessment of how well the students are doing when compared with a large sample of children of the same age and grade. Teachers have available a limited number of children in a class to compare how well that class or an individual student is progressing. Thus, commercially prepared tests are used to provide wider prediction and assessment of the pupils in a class.

There are other uses of tests besides those listed previously. A school district may wish to look at the general achievement level of its students. This district assessment may help the administration make suggestions for program improvement, purchasing additional instructional aids and equipment, or providing additional personnel. In addition, tests are used for research purposes to evaluate the effectiveness of a new program or to compare two modes of instruction. Any of the criteria to be described are relevant for these uses of tests as well.

• Factors to be Considered in Choosing a Test

Special Norms

A commercially prepared test usually offers the advantage of having been administered to a large number of children from a wide variety of rural and urban centers. Usually these tests have been administered to children of various social, racial, and ability levels. Thus, the test will have been "normed" on a population of children from more than just one class, school district, or state. A description of the norming population is critical for an interpretation of test scores. If one has a bright, urban class and the test has been normed with average, intercity children, the scores one's children obtain may indicate higher grade scores for that class than is a realistic assessment. If the reverse is true, that the test originally has been given to a large population of bright youngsters, the scores may be lower than is a realistic appraisal of one's students' current status.

It has been realized for some time now that in many situations national norms are not always the most appropriate. Lately some publishers have started to include norms specific to a particular geographic region or a particular educational reference group. This development is to be considered fortunate.

Standardization

Clear, standardized directions on how the test is to be administered are desirable. A set of directions that are concise and uniform will ensure that the results are not depressed or inflated because the directions left the procedure unclear. The students' scores will not be so useful if the test is given in a different way from the way it was given to the norming population.

Objectivity

A commercially prepared test also is intended to be objective; i.e., the score achieved should not be biased in some way by the tester or observer of the child's demonstration of what he knows. Encouragement, as everyone knows, can guide a pupil to a right answer. This is an excellent instructional technique as guided-discovery experiments have demonstrated. At times, however, one will want to know not how much a pupil can learn but how much he has learned and where he is now. An objective measure should enable one to determine this. As one shall see, tests vary in their objectivity.

Ease of Administration and Scorability

Given enough time and personnel, a teacher might collect extensive data about a child. This undertaking is not possible in most instances. Teachers want a test that makes reasonable demands in terms of the amount of time needed to administer the test so that children are not fatigued and also so the classroom instructional program may continue. In addition, tests that are difficult and tedious to score are sources of error and use far more teacher time than is desirable. Most achievement tests are designed to minimize the scoring time required of teachers.

Validity

A reading achievement test should sample the decoding, vocabulary, and comprehension skills taught. The titles of the tests should be an accurate description of the skills being tested. Evidence should be given that the skills of the test were measured with the norming population.

The test should also provide evidence that the skills measured are either a measure of current status or are of predictive value. One should know which tests can be used to predict success or failure in subsequent instruction. Not all tests provide this kind of evidence.

Three kinds of "validity" are important to consider. One is content validity. A test is said to have content validity to the degree its items are relevant both to the subject matter taught and the behaviors which the teaching is aiming to produce. Second is concurrent validity which compares the test behavior to current performance as measured in some other way. The third is predictive validity, which tells whether the score the child receives can be used to predict how well he will do in the future. A fourth, more difficult kind of validity, is construct validity, which refers to the psychological processes represented by the behaviors exhibited by the child during the test. For example, some reading tests claim that the comprehension skills measured on the test evaluate the child's ability to make inferences. Evidence should be offered by the manufacturer that the test items do measure this ability.

Reliability

When choosing a test one will want it to be a reliable measure of how much a child knows or how well he is able to apply his skills. The test results should not be a chance score with a child obtaining a high score by luck, guessing, or other factors. The test should not be constructed so that it gives the advantage to children who know only one thing well. The test should be constructed so that one has confidence that the score the child receives today will be similar to the score he would receive if the test were to be readministered to the same child tomorrow.

The Test Manual

It is the professional responsibility of the test maker to provide sufficient and appropriate evidence for the user to judge whether a test fits his purposes. Description of administration, norming, scoring, reliability, and validity should be provided in the user's manual. The authors have used the test manuals to evaluate the evidence provided and to assess in what ways the test can be recommended for use.

• How Can One Use Test Results?

Most achievement tests are group tests and provide a rough assessment of how a child compares with the norming sample. Such tests are not meant to be diagnostic, nor are they meant to give an accurate assessment of functional reading levels. They are a rough and ready means of grouping children for reading instruction. The grade placement score has little instructional value. The percentile score is more useful but again requires careful interpretation. If a test is used over a period of time, class norms may be built for a particular school district.

One of the greater *misuses* of the group standardized reading tests is the use of grade level norms as an indication of the level at which a student ought to be given reading instruction. Because of the nature of standardized tests, they are not appropriate for determining the reading level at which the youngster can profitably receive instruction. Standardized reading tests are developed from a group of items which are administered to a particular norming group; the grade norm is based on the average number of items that students get correct at a particular grade level. For example, a score of 6.0 may indicate only that a youngster who is just beginning sixth grade had 100 items correct. This score does not mean that the student who had 100 items correct can necessarily read 6.0 grade level material. The standardized tests were not meant to be criterion tests!

What we are suggesting is a procedure that might be used to determine the level at which a youngster may be given instruction on the basis of his standardized reading test score. Betts, in his 1942 book *Foundations of Reading Instruction,* suggested three functional reading levels. These functional reading levels are based on work that he and Patrick Killgallon had done. Credit also is given to Thorndike for the idea.

The three functional reading levels are as follows: 1) *independent* reading level, the level at which a youngster should be doing his leisure time reading; 2) *instructional* reading level, the level at which the youngster should be given reading instruction and should be learning in the content areas; and 3) *frustration* level, the reading level which is too difficult for the youngster and which will probably lead to negative conditioning to reading.

Usually, the various levels are defined in terms of performance on an informal reading inventory. The *independent level* is identified by 99 percent or better word call, 90 percent or better comprehension, and freedom from behavioral symptoms of tension and anxiety. The *instructional level* is identified by 95 percent or better correct word call, 75 percent or better comprehension, and only slight signs of anxiety. The *frustration level* implies 90 percent or less correct word call, less than 75 percent comprehension, and symptoms of nervousness, anxiety, and frustration.

A grade level score from a standardized reading test more often than not places a youngster at his frustration reading level. This relationship, of course, is dependent on the particular standardized test that is used and the particular material which is used for the informal reading inventory.

A procedure which might be used by classroom teachers to *determine the functional reading levels* (i.e., independent, instructional, and frustration) that correspond to *various scores on the standardized tests* would work something like this: The teacher would administer the usual standardized test to his class. To some of his students he would then administer an informal reading inventory (IRI), preferably based on the basal reader which he was using for instruction. Youngsters to be tested with the IRI would be selected from several points along the range of scores students achieved on the standardized tests. Students should be selected for testing at least from the bottom, middle, and top of the range of scores. Additional points on the range could be sampled if time allowed. The teacher would then determine the relationship between *various raw scores* on the standardized reading tests and the *functional reading levels on the informal reading inventory.* With data of this sort for several classes, he would find it unnecessary to readminister the informal reading inventory, being able to use the past performance of students to determine the levels at which they ought to be given instruction.

These procedures would enable a teacher to determine a functional reading level that would correspond to a particular raw score on a particular standardized reading test. For example, a student who scores 121 raw score points on a standardized reading test might have a fourth grade independent reading level, a fifth grade instructional reading level, and a sixth grade frustration level. Such knowledge would allow the teacher to utilize the standardized test scores to place each student at the instructional reading level where he would have the greatest opportunity to succeed. Two cautions, however, are in order: First, it is necessary to obtain estimates of the reliability of the IRI to be used and, second, one should always realize that the percentages which define the various levels are arbitrary. Finally, due to the unreliability of both instruments it would be necessary to check the various raw score "cut off" points by repeating the procedure suggested previously.

• Plan of this Reading Aid

Each test included in this review was assessed using the following outline:

I. Test Overview
   A. Title
   B. Author(s)
   C. Publisher
   D. Date of publication – original, revised
      1. Manual
      2. Test
   E. Level and Forms
      1. Grade level
      2. Individual or group
      3. Number of forms available
   F. Administration Time
   G. Scoring – hand or machine scorable
   H. Cost
      1. Question booklets – consumable or not
      2. Answer sheets
      3. Manual

II. Evaluation of Subtests and Items
   A. Description of subtests
      1. Given meaningful name – describe test adequately
      2. Is each subtest long enough to provide usable results?
      3. Sequential development of each subtest logical, and transitions smooth?
   B. Author's purpose reflected in selection of items
   C. Scoring ease and usability of tables
   D. Directions – clarity and level of language appropriate to grade level
   E. Design – format, currentness, printing, legibility, pictures
   F. Readability

III. Evaluation of Reliability and Validity
   A. Norming population
      1. Size
      2. Age, grade, sex
      3. Range of ability
      4. Socioeconomic level
      5. Date of administration
   B. Validity
      1. Content validity
         a. Face validity
         b. Logical or sampling validity
      2. Empirical validity
         a. Concurrent
         b. Predictive
      3. Construct validity
         a. Construct and theory of which construct is a part clearly defined
         b. Discriminant or convergent validity evidence
         c. Significant difference found in performance between groups which have varying degrees of this trait?
      4. Does reported validity appear adequate in relation to author's stated purpose? Why or why not?

Each test is described, and the strengths and weaknesses are delineated so that one may evaluate the test one's self. Each review was sent to the publisher for his reactions. In some cases, additional information was given the authors and this matter was included in the review. If the necessary data were not located in the manual but found elsewhere, the appropriate sources have been indicated. Finally, it should be the teacher who makes the final decision on the use of a test based on his program; the authors can only guide and suggest the criteria by which that decision might be made.

• What is the Responsibility of Test Publishers?

A test should be placed in the same category as a critical drug. A test should be used only after a careful study of its effects has been made. Evidence should be provided that the test (or drug) will do what it purports to do. Too many critical decisions are made about a child based on his test scores to use any test that is not a reliable and valid assessment of his ability to do the task described by the test. A teacher should insist that the test manufacturers provide him with the same reputable product that he would demand of a drug manufacturer who offers a new cure. It is better to use no test than to use an unreliable or invalid one. One finds that a number of tests are released before adequate data are available.

Many tests have not been studied sufficiently before they are put on the market for sale. One hopes the reader will note these deficiencies and realize how serious the action is to make an instructional, promotional, or evaluational decision about a child when it is not based on an accurate, stable, or predictive measure of his achievement.

Chapter 2

SELECTING A READING ACHIEVEMENT TEST

In Chapter 1 the characteristics of a good reading achievement test were discussed. Whether a particular test is a good test depends on how it is being used. For instance, some tests are fine as measures of general achievement but should never be used for purposes of diagnosis. When selecting a test, the prospective test user should first ask: "What do I want to find out? What kind of information should the test give me?" The merits of a test can only be judged in terms of its proposed usage.

Some important distinctions to be made in regard to testing purposes are the following:

- Do I want to measure achievement at a particular time, or do I want to measure changes in achievement?
- Am I primarily interested in the performance of a group of students (as an administrator might be), or is it the individual student I am primarily interested in (as a teacher might be)?
- Do I want to measure reading and achievement in a general sense, or do I have mastery of specific objectives in mind?
- Should the test provide for comparing the performance of my students with specific, clearly described norm groups?
- Do I want diagnostic information telling me on what areas of instruction I should focus?

The answers to these and similar questions will determine to what extent a test will be a good instrument for a particular test user. As much as possible the reviewers have kept these questions in mind when analyzing the merits of a given test. As a footnote, it may be added that in this book only general reading achievement tests are included. The issue of diagnostic utility will only be raised from time to time in terms of tests with distinct subtests that the test publisher states have diagnostic validity.

The test selection criteria indirectly referred to in the foregoing questions and in Chapter 1 are of a basic nature. They should play a major role in the choice of a test. Quite often, however, more than one test satisfies the basic criteria a test user has in mind, but there are other important points to consider, many of a very practical nature.

- How easily can the test be scored; is handscoring feasible; how long will it take to get machine-scorings returned?
- How long is the test? Is technical quality, such as a high reliability coefficient, achieved by an unreasonably large number of items?
- What is the risk that students will perform badly because of lack of clarity in format and directions?
- What does the test cost?

Practical issues such as these are far from trivial. They must, however, never outweigh more basic criteria about the fitness of a given test for the particular test purpose under consideration.

Chapter 3

TEST REVIEWS

• California Achievement Tests: Reading

Reviewed by Eugene Jongsma
Louisiana State University at New Orleans

Name of Test	**Subtests**	**Publication Date**
California Achievement Test: Reading	*Vocabulary* *Reading Comprehension*	1957
Revision Date	**Authors**	**Publisher**
1970	Ernest W. Tiegs Willis W. Clark	California Test Bureau/McGraw-Hill
Time		
50 Minutes		

Overview

The Reading section of the California Achievement Test (CAT-70) represents an extensive effort at revising and renorming the 1957 edition of this test. Over 85 percent of the test is composed of new items. Level 4 is designed for grades 6 through 9, and level 5, for grades 9 through 12. Two forms of the test, A and B, are available at each level.

At levels 4 and 5, the test consists of a vocabulary section of 40 items (10 minutes) and a comprehension section of 45 items (40 minutes). Three scores are available – vocabulary, comprehension, and total. Raw scores may be converted to grade equivalents, percentile ranks, stanines, or Achievement Development Scale Scores (ADSS). The ADSS is a scale of standard scores, ranging from 100 to 900, which is appropriate for making comparisons across forms and across levels of the test. The publishers wisely caution test users on the use of grade equivalent scores. In addition to the conventional hand scoring, Scoreze – a high-speed, self-scoring hand system – is available, as well as machine-scorable forms (CompuScan, IBM 1230, and Digitek).

Assistant superintendents, reading consultants, and other administrative personnel charged with the responsibility of directing a large-scale testing program would want to consult the *Test Coordinator's Handbook* and *Bulletin of Technical Data Number 1,* which contain additional information pertaining to the development, standardization, administration, and interpretation of the test.

Norms

The norms for this test were based on a nationwide sample of about 200,000 students representing both public and private schools. A total of

397 schools was included in the sample. The standardization sample was stratified on three factors: 1) geographic region (seven districts), 2) average enrollment per grade (small, medium, large), and 3) type of community (urban, rural, town, and other). The school districts participating in the standardization are listed in the *Test Coordinator's Handbook.*

No description is given of the norm group other than the three factors listed above. It would have been helpful to characterize the norm group in terms of sex, intelligence, socioeconomic status, or other demographic variables. As the information now exists, test users will be unable to determine to what extent their particular populations correspond with the standardization group. According to the publisher, follow-up questionnaires were used with each school to obtain descriptive information. These additional data are to be forthcoming in the *Technical Report.*

In the *Test Coordinator's Handbook,* the publisher encourages the use of local norms, especially for interpreting individual scores. Test users would be wise to follow this procedure, particularly if the local population differs substantially from the standardization group. Directions for preparing local norms are to be forthcoming in the *Technical Report.*

Reliability

Reliability data were obtained on a sample of 350 to 400 students per grade level from the standardization group referred to in the "norms" section. The sample of students used in the reliability study was drawn by systematic sampling so as to be representative of the norm group population. The data, provided in raw score form, include means, standard deviations, Kuder-Richardson-20 estimates, and standard errors of measurement for each grade and each level of the test.

The KR-20 estimates are fairly high, ranging from coefficients of .84 to .95, and reflect a high degree of internal consistency within the test. While desirable, internal consistency estimates, such as KR-20, ignore response variability of subjects and varying effects of testing conditions. No other reliability information is provided. Notably lacking are test-retest and parallel-form estimates. The publisher, however, does promise additional reliability data in the future *Technical Report.*

Test users should pay particular attention to the standard errors of measurement which are provided. They are useful in setting confidence limits around an individual's "true" score.

Validity

Content validity is reportedly based on a nationwide review of widely used reading tests and a study of curricular objectives and courses of study from a cross-section of states. However, the specific materials surveyed, their vintage, and the qualifications of the reviewers are not cited. A summary of reading objectives is presented which reads like most traditional reading methods textbooks. Test users should match their own instructional objectives with the actual tests to decide if the tests are appropriate evaluative instruments for the particular instructional programs. This writer believes that many of the objectives cited by the publisher are not measured by the test, e.g., "ability to read materials in specialized content areas, *adjusting rate and concentration to the purpose of their reading . . . .*" Indeed, one wonders whether the intended purpose of the overall test, "to measure progress in reading gained from various methods of instruction," is feasible or even desirable. No other type of validity, other than content validity, is reported.

Evaluation of Subtests and Items

The *Vocabulary* section consists of 40 items and is to be administered in 10 minutes. A stimulus word is presented in context, albeit limited, and the student must choose the best synonym from among four choices. The stimulus words represent various parts of speech and come from a range of subject areas.

The *Comprehension* section consists of 45 items and is to be administered in 40 minutes. For both levels 4 and 5, the first six items are intended to measure ability to use reference or study skills. While this is a valid aspect of reading instruction at the junior and senior high school level, six items are too few upon which to make an accurate and reliable judgment of a student's ability in this area.

The remaining portion of the *Comprehension* section consists of passages, arranged in an ascending order of difficulty, representing various types of materials – science, social studies, mathematics, and general. The passages are followed by four or five option multiple-choice items. Some vocabulary-type items are interspersed in the *Comprehension* section. Many of the comprehension items are specifically tied to the passage by the use of stems, such as "In this article, the writer's purpose is . . . ," and "the purpose of the third paragraph is . . . ." This tends to make items reading-dependent and serves to relieve a problem that has plagued the measurement of reading comprehension for years.

The *Technical Report* explains rather thoroughly how the time limits were developed. The time allowed should be adequate for most students. The test should not be considered "speeded" except for a very small number of students who are experiencing extreme reading difficulty.

Summary

Complete judgment regarding the *Reading* section of the newly developed California Achievement Test (CAT-70) will need to be reserved until more complete technical data become available. The information still needed includes: 1) a description of the materials and process used in developing the test objectives and content; 2) additional reliability data, particularly parallel-form and test-retest estimates; and 3) directions for preparing local norms.

In spite of the limitations cited in this review, this newly developed test represents a marked improvement over the older editions. Features such as the presentation of vocabulary words in context, the use of content area passages, a greater number of reading-dependent questions, and a more thorough discussion of development and standardization procedures add to the test's usefulness. The test is best suited as a survey measure of a junior or senior high school student's general reading ability.

• Cooperative English Tests – Reading Section

Reviewed by V. Michael Lahey
Virginia Commonwealth University

Name of Test	Subtests	Publication Date
Cooperative English Tests – Reading Section	*Vocabulary* *Comprehension*	1940
Revision Date	**Author**	**Publisher**
1960	C. Derrick D. P. Harris B. Walker	Educational Testing Service

Time
40

Overview

The Cooperative English Tests represent a 1960 revision and restandardization of older tests by the same name. These new tests measure achievement in two areas, reading and written expression. This review, however, will concern itself only with the reading tests.

The current tests are designed to replace the old forms R, RX, Y, and Z (Higher Level) and R, RX, T, Y, and Z (Lower Level). The newer tests are prepared at two levels with three forms at each level. High school students from grades 9 through 12 usually use one of the three forms at level two listed as 2A, 2B, and 2C. For above average students in Grade twelve, it is suggested that form 1A or 1B should be used. These two forms are suggested for average college freshmen and sophomores. Form 1C, also a college level test, is reserved for use only with admitted college freshmen and sophomores. The test manuals suggest that higher or lower level forms should be used with above or below average students.

Although the use of percentile bands for score reporting is more accurate than for grade equivalents, insufficient attention is devoted to the problem of score interpretation of very high or very low scores. Students in either of these two groups on any test are not accurately measured. Of particular concern are those whose scores place them in the very low group. A chance score (25 percent correct for four-choice, multiple-choice items) for the 60 items in the *Vocabulary* or *Speed of Comprehension* subtests would be 15 items correct. Taking the *Vocabulary* subtest as an example, this score results in a 2 through 15 percentile band in the ninth grade norm table and a .9 through 4 percentile band in the college sophomore norm table. This problem should be more forcefully presented than in the current set of manuals. Perhaps a mark or a line indicating the level of chance scores with some mention of the unreliability of scores below this level would be desirable.

Scoring can be done by machine (specific directions are included) or by hand. Hand scoring is accomplished by the use of overlays. Tables in the *Manual for Interpreting Scores* provide converted scores from their raw score equivalent. The converted scores are then used to find the appropriate percentile band in the norm table corresponding to the student's grade level. With the exception of college freshmen, all norm testing was done in the spring. College freshmen were tested in the fall. The *Manual for Interpreting Scores* provides a table which suggests the appropriate norm table for use when testing does not occur at the same time of year used in establishing the norms.

The significance of score differences is very simply found. If the two percentile bands being compared do not share at least one common percentile score, then their differences are significant.

The three manuals, *Directions for Administering and Scoring, Manual for Interpreting Scores,* and *Technical Report,* are all well done. There is no indication of any revision being made to any of the manuals since their 1960 publication date. Perhaps it would be in order to revise the section on validity in view of the many validation studies on this test conducted since 1960.

Norms

The tests were normed on both high school and college students. On the high school level norms were prepared for grades 9 through 12. The number of students included in the norming sample is not indicated. However, all students in grades 9 through 12 in the cooperating schools were tested. Slightly more than half of the 160 schools randomly selected produced usable results. Lack of cooperation or administrative errors removed the remainder from consideration. The manual points out the Southern states are overrepresented while the New England and Middle Atlantic states are underrepresented. An examination of the schools listed as participants would seem to indicate a greater number of rural or small town schools and a corresponding lack of schools in large metropolitan areas.

A 10 percent sample of the schools in the norm group was given the School and College Ability Tests to obtain an estimate of the verbal ability of the sample. Both groups had the same standard deviation and had mean scores within four converted-score points. The manner in which the 10 percent sample of schools was selected was not mentioned.

In norming the college level tests an effort was made to select a sample representative of the United States in regard to region and type of college. Colleges were divided into three geographic regions – North, South, and West. They were also divided into two levels: 1) liberal arts colleges and universities and 2) teachers' colleges, junior colleges, and technological schools. Originally 150 schools were contacted. Of these, 130 agreed to cooperate, but only 105 returned usable data. Only 78 colleges returned sophomore test data.

The authors recommend the development of local norms as being more informative. A complete, step-by-step procedure for establishing local norms is provided in the *Manual for Interpreting Scores.*

Reliability

Correlation with alternate forms was the method used to assess reliability. Two different forms were administered within a one-week period. By rotating the forms administered, it was possible to obtain reliability coefficients. Correlations of each form with the other two forms were averaged. *Total Reading* reliabilities ranged from .91 to .94. On the subtests of the various forms and levels correlations ranged from .71 to .89. The highest reliabilities of the subtests were consistently found to be on the *Vocabulary* subtest, .87 to .89. The lowest reliabilities were found on the *Level of Comprehension* subtest, .71 to .78, which is also the shortest subtest. The *Speed of Comprehension* subtests had reliability ranges from .81 to .87. Split half reliabilities were not computed, perhaps because a speed test contributed 40 percent to the total score. The test reliability would seem to be good for this test.

Validity

Validity is always a difficult topic to deal with. The authors feel that content validity is best assured by relying on well-qualified people to construct the tests. The authors further state that the validity of the revised tests should not be expected to be greatly different from the earlier versions. Only one study of the validity of the test is reported in the manuals while several studies are presented giving correlations of the earlier forms of the Cooperative English Tests with various criteria.

Evaluation of Subtests

Total Reading Score is derived from three scorings of two subtests. The 60 items on the *Vocabulary* subtest provide one score. The 60 items on the *Comprehension* subtest are scored in two ways to give two additional scores. The first 30 items are scored separately to provide a *Level of Comprehension* score while the total 60 items are scored to provide a *Speed of Comprehension* score.

The strategy behind the split score on the comprehension section is that the first 30 items could be completed by all students, making it a power test. On the other hand, the time limit for the full 60 items is such that few students can be expected to finish. This section then becomes a speed test.

The *Vocabulary* subtest presents a word in isolation followed by four choices. In view of recent linguistic findings that words derive their meanings from context, it would seem more desirable to use a context stem instead of a solitary word. Reading does not require the interpretation of words in isolation, but rather the ability to provide differing meanings for the same word in different contexts. The *Comprehension* subtest has a problem common to all tests of this type. Do they really measure reading comprehension? Several skills in addition to comprehension confound the scores. The ability to skim back over the item and locate information quickly is as important as the ability to understand or comprehend.

The directions are the same for all forms of the subtests so that both levels or all forms may be given at the same time. A trained test administrator is not required so long as the clear and concise directions are carefully followed.

Summary

The Cooperative English Tests measure achievement of high school and college students in reading and written expression. In general, the tests have been carefully constructed and provide a realistic means of interpreting scores.

Norming was conducted in the spring for high school students and college sophomores and in the fall for college freshmen. Some regional biases are reported, and some bias toward size of community is evident. However, results are close to those obtained on the School and College Ability Tests typically given to high school seniors. The reliability coefficients are satisfactorily high.

Reporting scores by the use of percentile bands rather than scores is an excellent idea and undoubtedly aids interpretation. It may prove confusing, however, to think of the percentile band as a single score as is done in the *Manual for Interpreting Scores.* A score falls in one place, but a band covers a wide range of scores and cannot be thought of as a single score.

This test, in spite of a few weaknesses, would seem to be a good test for measuring reading achievement of high school and college students.

• Davis Reading Test

Reviewed by Robert L. Schreiner

University of Minnesota

Name of Test	**Subtests**	**Publication Date**
Davis Reading Test	*Level of Comprehension* *Speed of Comprehension*	1957
Revision Date	**Authors**	**Publisher**
1961	F. B. Davis C. C. Davis	Psychological Corporation
Time		
40		

Overview

The Davis Reading Test was originally published in 1957 and revised in 1961 by the Psychological Corporation. There are two levels of the test. Series 1, is for average to above average pupils in grades 11 and 12 and for college freshmen. Series 2 is for pupils in grades 8, 9, 10, and 11. There are four parallel forms at each of the two levels of the test; hence, it may be used for repeated measures of secondary level reading ability.

Each series provides two separate but related scores. *The Level of Comprehension* subtest consists of the first 40 items of the test. The score on this subtest indicates the depth of understanding displayed by a pupil in reading materials ordinarily required for high school or college success. The second subtest, *Speed of Comprehension,* consisting of the first 40 plus the remainder of the items, is designed to determine how rapidly and accurately pupils must read and understand material in order to achieve academic success.

The authors state that the test is designed to measure the following five reading comprehension skills: 1) locating explicit or paraphrased information; 2) assimilating specific thoughts within a passage to grasp the central or main thought; 3) determining inferences regarding a passage and/or the author's purpose and his point of view; 4) recognizing tone, mood, and other literary devices used by an author; and 5) following the structure of a passage.

Pupils are allowed 40 minutes to complete the test. The actual testing session may take from 45 to 55 minutes. This feature makes the test quite practical for most secondary reading class periods. The examinee needs a test booklet, pencil, and an answer sheet to use the test.

The test can be scored either by hand or machine. Whichever procedure is used, the raw scores obtained by the pupils are corrected for guessing by using the following scoring formula: number right minus one-fourth the number wrong. The authors indicate that the purpose of the correction formula is to discourage wild guessing and to prevent sophisticated examinees from having an advantage over cautious or naive examinees in the *Speed of Comprehension* subtest. Pupils are told to omit questions rather than to guess wildly, but they are not told about the use of a formula to adjust the raw score for guessing.

The directions for the administration of the Davis Test are adequate and clear. Very little, if any, training is required to administer the test. The examiner's manual is extremely well organized. One problem, this reviewer noticed, dealt with the application of the guessing formula. The authors suggest that another person check each pupil's score for accuracy of calculation. This may be an impractical suggestion.

The reading passages cover a variety of subject matter areas. The content of the passages appears to be interesting and to reflect careful choices in order to represent all the subject matter areas appropriate for secondary pupils. The subtest *Speed of Comprehension* is a different way of measuring reading speed. The *Speed* score is determined by the total number of items correct for the entire test. While this procedure may be meaningful from a logical analysis point of view, it does not appear to be diagnostically meaningful. If a pupil shows weaknesses in speed of comprehension, it is not clear from his performance on the test what the teacher should do about this particular deficit. One thing seems clear: traditional speeded reading activities, those skills frequently taught in most secondary reading programs, would not be sufficient to improve a pupil's speed of comprehension score on the Davis Test. This skill seems to indicate that pupils should be provided with a purpose prior to reading each passage. Of course, purpose setting does not occur during the testing session.

Tables are provided in the examiner's manual so that raw scores may be converted into scaled scores. This procedure allows the consumer to make either group or individual comparisons. Hence, the teacher may be able to determine growth in reading ability for a large group of pupils or permit comparisons of growth of individual pupils. It also facilitates the interpretation of different scores between the separate subtests of the reading test.

The authors' purposes for the selection of the items of the test are presented in the examiner's manual and are based on their careful research and survey of the literature related to reading comprehension skills. The authors initially located over a hundred reading comprehension skills and indicated that many comprehension skills are related to mechanics of reading while others are incapable of measurement by objective test items. The original list of one hundred was reduced to nine clusters, called operational skills, employed in comprehension in reading. The first two of the skills are related to verbal aptitude. Because of the pervasive nature of word *memory,* it was decided not to provide a separate measure of vocabulary in the Davis Tests. The remainder was grouped into the five categories previously mentioned. The following list provides the approximate number of items per grouping for each of the four forms of the test: 1) locating specific information (20), 2) locating central thought (20), 3) determining inferences and authors' purposes (20), 4) finding literary techniques (10), and 5) following passage structure (10). Originally, 650 items were constructed to measure these five reading comprehension skills. These items were then administered, with an unlimited amount of time, to pupils to determine which items were suitable. Finally, 320 items were selected for the construction of the four forms of Series 1. A similar procedure was used to select items for Series 2.

A teacher may wish to examine the pupil response patterns on each of the categories upon which the test is constructed. The skill category for each of the items on both forms of the Davis Reading Tests may be obtained by writing to the Psychological Corporation.

Norms

Percentile norms for each of the subtests of the Davis Test are provided in the examiner's manual. The norms for the Series 1 tests are based on the testing in 1957 of over 18,000 pupils in grades 11, 12, and college freshmen. Eighteen colleges and universities administered the tests to their entering freshmen, and 29 high schools contributed norm samples for grades 11 and 12. These institutions were well distributed geographically. However, it appears that the high school sample could have included schools of medium or small size and pupils from lower socioeconomic sections of the population. Percentile norms for Series 2 (grades 8 to 11) are provided based on test results administered to 21,000 pupils in 1961. Fifty-two high schools contributed norm samples for these grades levels. Again, this norm sample was drawn from larger metropolitan areas with a smaller percentage of pupils from lower socioeconomic areas than might be desirable.

Reliability

Reliability coefficients for Series 1 of the Davis Test were based on the administration of two equivalent forms of the test with a three-week interval between administrations for pupils in grades 11 and 12 and on a one-week interval for college freshmen. Reliability coefficients for Series 2 forms were based on the administration of two forms of the test with two to four weeks between administrations for grades 8 through 11.

The average reliability coefficients reported for Series 2, *Level of Comprehension* subtest, are .84 (grade 8), .84 (grade 9), .78 (grade 10), and .77 (grade 11). For Series 1 they are .74 (grade 11), .77 (grade 12), and .80 (college freshmen).

The average reliability coefficients reported for the *Speed of Comprehension* subtests, Series 1, are .91 (grade 8), .91 (grade 9), .86 (grade 10), and .86 (grade 11). For Series 2 they are .84 (grade 11), .85 (grade 12), and .88 (college freshmen). These reliability coefficients compare favorably with other current measures of reading ability.

Validity

The Davis Reading Test was designed, by careful analysis, to measure the five reading comprehension skills previously mentioned. The authors refer the user to the results of several factorial studies that substantiate these same reading comprehension skills. They indicate that the *Level of Comprehension* score, based on the first 40 items, measures only accuracy or depth of comprehension. They further indicate the pupils who do not complete the first 40 items are likely to be reading disability cases and that these pupils should be referred for individual diagnosis and remedial work. The *Speed of Comprehension* subtest is designed to measure both accuracy and depth of understanding plus speed of reading. The pupil's score on all 80 items is used to determine *Speed of Comprehension.*

Upon inspection of some of the items, one finds many detailed questions that appear to hinder speed. Some of the questions seem to require the pupil to retain a substantial number of details to obtain the correct answer. Frequently, this reviewer had to return to the reading passage and count objects or events in order to answer a question. For example, "How many plants gotten by Europe from America are mentioned in the passage? a) eleven, b) eight, c) seven, d) four, or e) six."

Data are presented to indicate the predictive usefulness of the Davis Test. The test was administered to a sample of over 1,700 college students. The results of the test were compared to the obtained first semester English course grade. Correlation coefficients between these two measures were obtained, and they ranged from .36 to .57 with a median of .46. Each pupil's first semester grade point average was also compared with his performance on the reading test. These coefficients ranged from .37 to .56, with a median of .46. Data on the predictive validity of the test at the high school level are also presented. Individual pupil performance at grades 11 and 12 on the Davis Test was compared to the grade achieved in English. These correlation coefficients ranged from .15 to .64 with a median of approximately .46.

Correlation data are presented comparing the results of pupil performance on the Davis Reading Test and other similar tests. The following correlation coefficients between the Davis Test and other tests are reported: 1) STEP Reading, .76 (college freshmen); 2) DAT Verbal Reasoning, .76; 3) ITBS Reading, .77 (Grade 8); 4) COOP Reading Comprehension, .75 (Grade 10); and 5) ITED Composite, .77 (Grade 10).

Evaluation of subtests

In order for a standardized test of reading ability to be truly useful, it must provide diagnostically relevant information to the test consumer. The subtest scores that the pupils receive must give some clues so that teachers may be provided with appropriate teaching or remedial alternatives. For example, if a pupil receives a substantially lower scaled score on the *Level of Comprehension* subtest than on the *Speed of Comprehension* subtest of the Davis Test, what information does this result provide to the teacher? What teaching methods and materials must the teacher now employ to help the pupil increase his level of reading comprehension? This kind of information is not provided by the authors.

A similar situation exists if a pupil's score is lower on the *Speed of Comprehension* subtest. The authors take great pains to distinguish between reading speed as traditionally defined and speed of comprehension, i.e., rapid reading with thorough understanding. However, how does one teach pupils to read rapidly with increased accuracy? The authors do not provide suggestions.

Most secondary reading programs provide systematic instruction for pupils aimed at the improvement of reading speed measured in words per minute, level of vocabulary, and comprehension skills. The kinds of instructional activities associated with reading improvement programs at the secondary levels do not appear to be directly measured by the Davis test. Reading speed, it seems to this reviewer, is more appropriately measured if passages of greater length are used that deal with a variety of disciplines represented within the high school curriculum, followed by a series of comprehension questions. Secondary pupils rarely read short passages as used in the Davis Tests and then answer five to six multiple-choice questions about them.

Summary

The authors indicate that accuracy of reading comprehension is much more dependent on ability to associate word meanings correctly than any other mental ability. No specific measure of vocabulary ability, however, is included as a part of the test. The authors indicate that memory of word meanings is so pervasive an ability that it was decided not to measure it separately. One could argue that the processes underlying reading comprehension are even more pervasive and, therefore, they defy measurement. This reviewer feels that some assessment of a pupil's vocabulary ability is important diagnostic information for the secondary reading teacher.

The skills assessed by the Davis Reading Test appear to be globally defined by the authors and, hence, are of limited diagnostic use to the teacher of secondary reading. The test is extremely well constructed and exemplary in all aspects of treatment of statistical data. This reviewer would suggest, however, that the test be used at the secondary level as a survey measure to assess general reading ability. It appears to have limited diagnostic value.

• Diagnostic Reading Tests

Reviewed by Eugene Jongsma
Louisiana State University at New Orleans

Name of Test	**Subtests**	**Publication Date**
Diagnostic Reading Tests	*Survey Section* *Diagnostic Battery*	1947
Revision Date	**Authors**	**Publisher**
Varies with subtests	Committee on Diagnostic Reading Tests	Committee on Diagnostic Reading Tests
Time		
Varies with subtests		

Overview

The Diagnostic Reading Tests are the product of an ambitious effort by the Committee on Diagnostic Reading Tests to develop a survey and diagnostic battery appropriate for students from kindergarten through the college freshman year. The various components of the test battery are outlined below.

A. Survey Section: Upper Level (Forms A through H)
   1. Rate of Reading
   2. Vocabulary
   3. Comprehension
   4. Total Comprehension

B. The Diagnostic Battery (Forms A and B)
   Section I: Vocabulary
      1. English
      2. Mathematics
      3. Science
      4. Social Studies
      5. Total
   Section II: Comprehension
      Part 1. Silent
      Part 2. Auditory
   Section III: Rates of Reading
   Section IV: Word Attack
      Part 1. Oral
      Part 2. Silent

The *Survey Section* is intended to be used as an independent measure of general reading ability or as a screening instrument to identify students in need of further diagnostic testing. The multiple sections of the *Diagnostic Battery* are designed to provide a more specific assessment of the various aspects of the reading process, i.e., vocabulary, comprehension, rate, and word attack. Each section of the battery comes as a separate test booklet with a separate set of directions. Raw scores may only be converted to percentile ranks as the committee is firmly opposed to the use of grade norms or grade equivalent scores.

Norms

Except for *Section II, Silent and Auditory Comprehension,* all norms are included in a separate booklet of consolidated norm tables entitled *The Diagnostic Reading Tests: Norms* (1967). This booklet must be ordered in addition to the tests.

The normative data presented by the committee are woefully inadequate for a number of reasons. First, one set of norms is provided for all forms of each section or subtest. The publisher justifies this lack by claiming that the forms of each subtest are equivalent. Yet, no proof of equivalency is given. Second, many of the subtest norms are extremely outdated; some are twenty years old. Third, on some subtests, particularly certain sections of the *Diagnostic Battery,* the norms are based on too small a population to be representative or reliable. Last, and most important, a test user has no information as to the kinds of groups on which the tests were standardized. Thus, it is virtually meaningless for a test user to interpret his students' results with the norms provided. In the norm booklet mentioned, the committee states, "The characteristics of this (standardization) population must be defined so that a norm group may be selected which is similar to the particular group being tested" (p.5). Yet, no information concerning the aptitude, ability, socioeconomic status, or geographic origins of the norm group is provided by the committee.

Careful examination of the norm tables reveals another deficiency. It appears that some sections of the battery are too difficult for seventh graders and possibly for some eighth graders; consequently, the sections do not provide an appropriate level assessment of their reading abilities. For example, a seventh grader receiving a chance score (a raw score of 10 out of 50, five option items) on the social studies part of the *Section I: Vocabulary Test* would rank at the 44th percentile for his grade level. This example clearly shows that this particular subtest is not adequately measuring the vocabulary skills of most seventh graders.

In light of the inadequacies identified in this section, test users would be wise to bypass the available norms and accept the committee's offer to compute their local norms without charge.

Reliability

The reliability data, also presented in *The Diagnostic Reading Tests: Norms,* are insufficient. A median coefficient based on the Kuder-Richardson-21 procedure is presented for each subtest and test totals. Although the coefficients are fairly high, ranging from .80 to .97, it is not clear just what has been "averaged." It is also likely that the KR-21 estimates are inappropriate for some subtests on which speed is a factor. As with the norms, the group used to obtain the reliability estimates is not described. The size of this sample is not even given. The reliability estimates that are presented are meant to apply to all forms of the test. No estimate of alternate-form reliability is available.

One subtest with questionable reliability is *Section III: Rates of Reading Test.* The publisher does, however, caution that if this test is to be used in individual diagnosis, both forms should be given, one immediately following the other.

Validity

Perhaps the greatest technical weakness of the Diagnostic Reading Tests is the complete lack of evidence pertaining to their validity. The test battery is promoted and sold as a "diagnostic" instrument, yet no data are provided which demonstrate the independence of the subtests. Subtest intercorrelations are lacking.

Perhaps more fundamental is the absence of a rationale for construction of the test. There does not seem to have been a systematic plan for developing the test objectives, choosing the test material, and selecting the test items. At least no such scheme is explicitly stated.

Instead of providing the necessary validity information in the test manuals, the publisher has shifted the burden of proof to the test consumer by encouraging him to locate and read research related to the use of the Diagnostic Reading Tests. Although it is desirable for test users to familiarize themselves with such literature, the test publisher has a definite responsibility to provide sufficient information that will allow a test user to make accurate judgments concerning the usefulness and interpretation of the test, according to the *Standards for Educational and Psychological Tests and Manuals.*

Evaluation of Subtests and Items

The *Survey Section* is designed primarily as a screening instrument and as such yields the following scores: 1) *Rate of Reading,* 2) *Vocabulary,* 3) *Comprehension,* and 4) *Total Comprehension.* The rate subtest measures the student's usual rate of reading story-type material. Twenty multiple-choice comprehension questions follow the passage but do not yield a separate score. The *Vocabulary* subtest consists of 60 items and is to be completed in 10 minutes. Definitions are given in context, and the student must select from among five the one word which has been defined. The *Comprehension* subtest is comprised of 4 passages and 20 multiple-choice items which must be completed in 15 minutes. The items appear to measure a variety of skills. The *Total Comprehension* score is a misnomer since 60 of the 100 items upon which this score is based are vocabulary items. It should be considered a "total test" score instead.

The *Section I: Vocabulary* test is made up of four sections – English, Mathematics, Science, and Social Studies. Each section contains 50 items of the same format used in the *Vocabulary* subtest of the *Survey Section.* In fact, several of the items are identical to those used in the Survey test. Time is likely to be an important factor for many students on this test.

The *Section II: Comprehension* test consists of 16 passages and 50 multiple-choice comprehension items. The test may be administered as a silent comprehension test or as an auditory or listening comprehension test. No norms are available, however, for the latter procedure.

The *Section III: Rates of Reading* test consists of two passages followed by multiple-choice questions. On the first passage, students are directed to read at their "regular" rates while on the second passage they are encouraged to read as rapidly as possible without a loss in understanding. No percentile norms are available for the comprehension aspect of this test.

The *Section IV: Word Attack* test is composed of oral and silent parts. For the oral part, which must be administered individually, the student reads a series of passages which gradually increase in difficulty while the test administrator records substitutions, omissions, and repetitions. This work is followed by the pronunciation of isolated words in a series of three word lists. The silent part of the test measures the students' abilities to match words that have similar sounds and the abilities to recognize the numbers of syllables in selected words.

Summary

The Diagnostic Reading Tests represent an extensive battery of subtests, each with its own test booklet and its own manual of directions. Unfortunately, some of the information presented in the manuals is conflicting and often misleading, creating a complex and often confusing array of test materials. This problem could be alleviated somewhat by consolidating the directions for the various parts of the diagnostic battery into one booklet.

Technically, the tests leave much to be desired. No evidence of validity is provided. The reliability data are insufficient, and useful descriptive information, such as means, standard deviations, and standard errors of measurement for the norm groups, is not available.

The test is better suited for high school students than junior high pupils. The *Survey Section* may be used as a measure of general reading ability, but the diagnostic utility of the battery is doubtful.

In light of the inadequacies and limitations raised in this review, test consumers would do well to consider other tests on the market which offer more substantial and comprehensive technical data.

In a real sense the Committee on Diagnostic Reading Tests is a victim of the times. Started in the 1940s as a noble effort by a handful of dedicated professionals, it now finds itself competing with the vast resources and technical expertise of the test giants which have emerged in the field of measurement.

• Gates-MacGinitie Reading Tests

Reviewed by William E. Blanton

Indiana University

Name of Test	**Subtests**	**Publication Date**
Gates-MacGinitie Reading Tests	*Speed and Accuracy Test* *Vocabulary Test* *Comprehension Test*	1965, 1970
Authors	**Publisher**	**Time**
Arthur L. Gates Walter H. MacGinitie	Teachers College Press	44 minutes

Overview

The Gates-MacGinitie Reading Tests represent a new edition standardized in 1965 and 1969. This series replaces the Gates Primary and Advanced Primary Reading Tests and the Gates Reading Survey. Included in this eight-test series are tests for grade levels from kindergarten through grade 12. The purpose of this review is to cover Survey E for grades 7 through 9 and Survey F for grades 10 through 12.

Survey E and Survey F consist of three subtests: *Speed and Accuracy, Vocabulary,* and *Comprehension.* Three forms are available for Survey E; two forms are available for Survey F. Both surveys are also available in hand-scored or machine-scored editions.

The authors are very careful to assist test users in making correct interpretations of test results. The *Technical Supplement* provides tables for converting raw scores into standard scores and percentiles, interpreting differences between subtest scores, and estimating reading test gains. Norms for the beginning, middle, and end of each grade level are also provided.

The significance for differences between subtest scores is determined on the basis of probability. If differences between two subtest scores occur more than fifteen times out of a hundred, the obtained scores should be used in planning reading instruction. Similarly, differences in reading test gains are considered significant when they occur more than fifteen times out of a hundred.

Total reading score is determined by averaging the standard scores of the subtests. The authors correctly point out that, when determining averages, it is poor practice to sum and divide raw scores since they are not based on an equal-interval scale. It should also be pointed out that the authors deemphasize grade equivalents which are rarely accurate for high school students.

The American Psychological Association's *Standards for Educational and Psychological Tests and Manuals* considers it essential that a test manual indicate the qualifications required to administer and interpret a test properly. It is interesting to note that the Gates-MacGinitie Reading Tests manual makes no attempt to do this. Moreover, the *Teacher's Manual* and the *Technical Supplement* suffer the same deficiencies as those of many other reading tests: a discussion of the uses of the test and of the reading behaviors sampled is not provided. The *Teacher's Manual* suggests that the teacher may best understand the tasks imposed and meaning of the resulting scores by reading the test and carefully considering what is involved in getting correct answers. This suggestion is valid to the extent that classroom teachers have the expertise to make an item analysis of the test. Indeed, it is desirable that the test user familiarize himself with the test and its uses. The test publisher, however, has the responsibility of providing the user with information necessary for making responsible decisions concerning the use and interpretation of the test.

Norms

The normative data presented by the publisher is inadequate for a number of reasons. First, according to the *Technical Manual,* the norming population was "... carefully selected on the basis of size, geographical locations, average educational level, and average family income." These criteria, however, are not explicitly defined. It is interesting to note, though, that testing was carried out in "... schools, judged by school officials to be representative of the community as a whole." Second, demographic characteristics of the norming population are not adequately described. Third, norms for the hand-scored editions appear to be based on too small an "n" to be representative or reliable. Consequently, it is extremely difficult for the test user to interpret test results with the normative data provided. Users of the test, therefore, might insure the most meaningful interpretation of test results by obtaining local norms.

Reliability

Both split-half and alternate-form reliability coefficients are reported by subtests for machine-scored editions of the tests. In every instance, these data are acceptable. On the other hand, no reliability data are presented for hand-scored editions. In light of this inadequacy, test users would be wise to compute reliability coefficients for local populations or have the tests machine-scored.

Validity

Validity evidence for the tests is limited. The tests, however, do appear to have face validity. Users of the test should be aware of the fact that the manual fails to provide a description of the curriculum content which the tests purport to measure. More important, there is no evidence that the subtests were developed according to the content of reading programs. Before using these tests, consequently, the user should examine the objectives of his reading program and compare these to the content of the tests.

Correlations between subtests and Lorge-Thorndike Verbal IQ scores are reported. In general, these correlations reveal a high degree of relationship between *Vocabulary* and *Comprehension* scores and verbal IQ scores. *Speed and Accuracy* test scores, on the other hand, are less related to verbal IQ scores. In short, the correlations between subtests scores and verbal IQ scores lend credence to the argument that there is a high degree of relationship between group measures of reading behavior and group measures of verbal IQ.

Evaluation of Subtests and Items

According to the authors, "The *Speed and Accuracy Test* provides an objective measure of how rapidly students can read with understanding." Items for the *Speed and Accuracy Test* are 36 short paragraphs ending in a question or an incomplete sentence. Students indicate their responses by selecting one of four words presented. Two scores are reported: *Speed*, the number of items attempted, and *Accuracy*, the number of correct items. Time allowed for this subtest is four minutes.

The stated purpose of the *Vocabulary* subtest is "to sample the students' reading vocabulary." This subtest consists of 50 items in which the student matches a test word with one of five words that follow. In both surveys, the item progression for this subtest appears to be from easy to difficult. A time limit of 15 minutes is allowed for this section.

According to the authors, the stated purpose of the *Comprehension Test* is to measure, "students' abilities to read complete prose passages with understanding." This section contains 21 passages with two to four words per paragraph deleted for a total of 52 deletions. For each deletion, the student selects the answer which best conforms to the meaning of the whole passage from a word list of five alternatives. For both surveys, the average difficulty for the passages to be read appears to progress from the easiest to most difficult. Time allowed for this section is 25 minutes.

In sum, the names assigned the three subtests are functional and accurately describe the actual tests. It should be noted, however, that the *Speed and Accuracy* items vary in what is required to answer an item. For instance, some items require inference as well as matching of a definition with the correct word. In addition, the *Comprehension Test* apparently taps only one type of comprehension: the ability to use context clues in conjunction with the overall meaning of the passage.

Summary

The Gates-MacGinitie Reading Tests, Survey E and Survey F, are a set of group reading tests based on recent normative data. The tests yield a measure of general reading achievement for students from grades 7 through 12. In general, the tests are well constructed and provide useful information for evaluating growth, screening students for further diagnostic testing, and organizing pupils for instruction. The use of the tests for making classroom decisions, such as diagnosing specific reading skills, is limited even though the authors suggest that teachers interpret test scores through item analysis.

The tests have been normed for periodic assessment, and the subtests and total test scores are reliable. Still, the test user should examine the validity for measuring the objectives of a specific reading program. It should also be noted that limitations are found in the description of the norming population and in the failure to report reliabilities for hand-scored editions. Thus, the development of local norms would aid in the interpretation of test scores.

• Iowa Silent Reading Tests

Reviewed by Ronald Johnson
Wisconsin State University at River Falls

Name of Test	Subtests	Publication Date
Iowa Silent Reading Tests	*Vocabulary* *Comprehension* *Directed Reading* *Reading Efficiency*	1929
Revision Date		**Publisher**
1973		Harcourt Brace Jovanovich

At the time of this writing a thoroughly revised edition of the Iowa Silent Reading Tests (ISRT) was being prepared. The publisher made available the detailed specifications used in developing the tests and copies of the restricted (item-analysis) edition, 1971, tests at each of the three levels. It was expected that this edition would conform closely to the final published form of the tests. Since this edition was for item-analysis purposes only, neither a test administrator's manual nor a technical manual was available. This article, therefore, might be more appropriately called a preview rather than a review of this test.

Overview

Three levels of the Iowa Silent Reading Tests are available: Level I for grades 6 through 9, Level II for grades 9 through 12 (average readers), and Level III for grades 11 through 14 (superior readers). Levels I and II each have four subtests: *Vocabulary, Comprehension, Directed Reading,* and *Reading Efficiency. Directed Reading* is divided into "Part A: Locating Information" and "Part B: Skimming and Scanning." Level III has three subtests: *Vocabulary, Comprehension,* and *Reading Efficiency.*

Norms – Reliability – Validity

No data on these important topics were available at the time of this review. This reviewer would strongly urge that any prospective user of this test obtain a technical manual from the publisher before purchasing the tests.

Evaluation of Subtests

In the *Vocabulary* subtest at all three levels, the student is required to select a synonym for a stimulus word from among four distractors. The words included in these subtests have been selected to represent general reading vocabulary. This procedure represents a marked change from the earlier edition of the ISRT where the words were selected as "significant words in four high school subjects."

The *comprehension* subtests, for the most part, follow the common format of a series of multiple-choice questions on selections which increase in length and complexity as the student progresses through the test. The content of the selections is varied; the great majority, however, seem to be oriented toward the social studies. The final selection of the *Comprehension* subtests at each level varies somewhat from this format. In Levels I and II the student is directed to "read and study" a rather lengthy selection. He then turns the page and answers 16 questions without looking back at the selection. It does not appear that the different type of recall assumed to be required in this task will be scored separately. In Level III the student is directed to read two short selections before answering the multiple-choice questions which contrast the views of the two writers and shift back and forth with questions on the separate selections. It is not clear to this reviewer just what comprehension skills this selection is designed to measure; nevertheless, whatever it measures is not scored separately, and its contribution will probably be mixed in with the rest of the items in this subtest.

The *Directed Reading* subtest is a part of Levels I and II only. "Part A: Locating Information" attempts to measure the student's reading-study skills by stressing the use of a dictionary and locating information in a variety of sources. "Part B: Skimming and Scanning" consists of a factual article of the kind found in most encyclopedias. Only the article, including charts and graphs, is printed in the test booklet. The multiple-choice questions are printed in the student's separate answer sheet. The student is directed to read each question and to "glance over" the article in order to answer the questions. He is specifically told not to try to read the entire article. In this writer's experience with the *Directed Reading* subtest of the earlier edition, these directions cannot be stressed too strongly. Invariably, a number of students will follow the learning set established over the years by similar tests and by the previous subtests in this test: The change in procedure does not register; they begin to read the entire article from beginning to end, and they answer no questions before the time runs out. While a low score for these students does indicate that they do not follow directions, their score is not related to the reading skills of skimming and scanning that the subtest was designed to measure. The directions in this revision are more pointed than those of earlier editions of the ISRT; this reviewer, however, suggests that the test administrator place special emphasis on the changed format or that he consider administering this subtest first when a higher percentage of the students are listening to the directions. There are simpler, more dramatic demonstrations of the student's inability to follow directions than is offered by an invalid score on this subtest.

The *Reading Efficiency* subtest is included in Levels I, II, and III. Like the questions for skimming and scanning in Levels I and II, the question for this subtest are printed on the student's answer sheet rather than in the test booklet. This subtest represents the only deviation from a four-distractor, multiple-choice format in the entire battery. The deviation is slight. The student is presented with a connected passage; at certain breaks in the passage he is to mark which of three words fits the context (a three-distractor, multiple-choice modified cloze procedure). How often words are omitted varies from the fourteenth to the thirty-seventh word. Some tests using cloze procedure require the student to read beyond the blank in order to gain enough information to supply the correct response. The ISRT avoids this problem by having every blank occur at the end of a sentence. Even though the cloze procedure technique for measuring reading comprehension was greatly modified in preparing this subtest, the resulting format may well be too artificial to yield a useful estimate of either the student's rate of reading or of his comprehension.

Summary

Only item-analysis copies of the Iowa Silent Reading Tests, Restricted Edition, 1971, were examined. For this reason manuals were not available at the time this review was written.

Three levels of the test are available covering the range from grades 6 through 14. The two lower levels have subtests measuring *Vocabulary, Reading Comprehension, Directed Reading,* and *Reading Efficiency.* Level III measures *Vocabulary, Reading Comprehension,* and *Reading Efficiency.* Each of the tests seems to be carefully prepared and easy to use. Three important questions are not answered because the data were not available when this review was written: 1) Is the norm population adequate for the user's student population? 2) Are the scores yielded by this test valid? 3) Are they reliable?

It is most unfortunate that with the long-needed revision of the ISRT, it has lost its uniqueness. The older test attempted to measure skills directly related to achievement in school subject areas. The revision seems to have become almost indistinguishable from all of the other reading tests available, both in terms of what it measures and in the items it uses.

• The Metropolitan Achievement Tests: Reading, Advanced Level

Reviewed by Joe Peterson
The University of Georgia

Name of Test
Metropolitan Achievement Tests: Reading, Advanced Level

Revision Date
1970

Subtests
Word Knowledge
Reading

Authors
W. W. Durost
H. H. Bixler
S. W. Wrightstone
G. A. Prescott
I. H. Balow

Publication Date
1959

Publisher
Harcourt Brace Jovanovich

Overview

The Metropolitan Achievement tests, of which the Metropolitan Reading tests are a part, have been published in a fourth edition, effective with the 1970 copyright. Virtually all new material has been created for these tests, and the *Reading* subtest at the advanced level has at least one selection relevant to the Black culture. As was the case previously, the Metropolitan Reading tests are available as a separate part of the total battery and contain two subtests: *Word Knowledge* and *Reading.* Three scores are generally computed from these two subtests and are confusingly labeled *Word Knowledge, Reading,* and *Total Reading.* As might be expected, the *Total Reading* score includes the number of correct responses from both subtests.

One of the strong points of the Metropolitan Reading tests has been the clarity of the *Teachers' Directions* and the *Teachers' Handbook.* These continue to be well written and will provide good information to the users of the tests. Nothing is taken for granted in these manuals; indeed, the discussion begins in the *Teachers' Handbook* with the candid question "Why test?" and proceeds from that point to detailed directions for administering the tests and for interpreting the results once the testing has been completed. It is commendable that the publishers put their tests into a proper perspective in that the tests should be thought of as only one of many sources of information to be considered in trying to understand pupils.

Norms

Contrary to usual practices, standardization procedures have been carried out on all three forms of the test rather than standardizing one form and equating the others to it. Since testing in the schools is almost evenly divided between fall and spring, the test constructors decided to standardize the tests at two different times during the school year rather than once, as has been the practice in the past. Accordingly, Forms G and H were standardized in October and Form F in April, each form being administered to a balanced sample of about 7,000 students in grades 7 and 8 and, for Forms G and H, about 4,000 students in Grade 9. Studies of equivalency were conducted during the spring standardization program.

Four types of derived scores are provided for the tests: standard scores, percentile ranks, stanines, and grade equivalents. According to the *Handbook,* the basic use of standard scores is for measuring growth within an area (Did Johnny exhibit any growth in reading?) whereas stanines and percentile ranks provide a means for comparing subtest scores in different areas (Is Johnny's reading achievement grossly different from his word knowledge?). The familiar grade equivalent score is downgraded for its inherent inaccuracies and ease in misinterpretation when dealing with individual scores. Emphasis has been placed on the use of the more sensible stanines in interpreting comparisons between subtests in order to help avoid the overly precise connotation of other derived scores. This emphasis should be heeded.

According to information provided by the publisher, all levels of the 1958 edition and all levels of the 1970 edition were given to comparable groups of unspecified size. A table was compiled from these five batteries which shows comparable grade equivalent scores on the two editions of the tests so that the results of the old and new editions can be compared. Indications are that a grade equivalent of 9.4 on the 1958 *Word Knowledge* test is equivalent to 9.0 on the 1970 edition whereas a 9.4 on the 1958 *Reading* subtest would come out the same (i.e., 9.4) on the 1970 edition. Most of the rest of the *Word Knowledge* scores below 8.0 and the *Reading* subtest scores seem to fluctuate from almost exact equivalence to instances where the 1958 edition appears to be the harder version by as much as 0.5 years; e.g., an ability which would have earned a 5.9 on the 1958 *Reading* subtest would probably have earned a 6.4 on the 1970 *Reading* subtest. Although the differences between the two tests do not all vary in the same direction, the comparison suggests that the average junior high reader of 1970 is slightly better than the average junior high reader of twelve years ago. Such comparisons, however, should be interpreted cautiously since they are based on the assumption that norming samples of the two editions are drawn from the parent population in exactly the same way and that the changes in the content of the material the pupils read for the test, when mixed with changes in our culture, are immaterial variables.

Reliability

Split-half reliabilities have been computed for both fall and spring standardization groups for each of the three grades on which it was standardized. The range is from .92 to .97 for the tests, individually and combined, therefore indicating high internal consistency. No data on alternate form reliability were available at the time of this review.

Validity

Validity of the tests is defined in terms of content validity. A description of the process whereby the content of the tests was decided upon has been published. Users of the test, however, will need to survey the content of the tests to determine the fit of the tests to their curriculum. A brochure, *Content Outlines,* is provided for this purpose.

Evaluation of Subtests and Stems

In the final analysis, the worth of the Metropolitan Reading Tests as tests of reading ability depends upon the user's definition of reading. Given a broad definition of reading, the tests have less than adequate worth; given a more restrictive definition, however, the tests do an adequate job of measuring reading skill. A description of the tests should illustrate this matter.

The *Total Reading* test is made of two parts, a *Word Knowledge* subtest and a *Reading* subtest. The *Word Knowledge* subtest consists of 50 words in isolation – from the areas of a) general information, b) social studies, c) humanities, d) science and mathematics, and e) antonyms – for each of which the pupils have to select one of four meanings. To the casual observer, this test would appear to be measuring general knowledge rather than reading ability.

The *Reading* subtest consists of forty-five questions based on seven selections varying in length from two to five paragraphs. The types of questions asked are classified into four types and are represented in the following proportions in Form F: words in context, 11/45; literal questions, 7/45; inference questions, 23/45; and main thought questions, 4/45. It should be noted that this portion of the test does a good job of measuring the *higher* cognitive process reading abilities and does it with materials covering the sciences, social sciences, and humanities, all of which are expository in nature.

Complete as these *Reading* tests seem, however, they do not measure rate nor include any materials to check reading ability in the literary materials usually found in the English-language arts curriculum, nor are any of the traditional work-study skills evaluated. If, however, the whole Metropolitan Achievement Test battery has been given, the enterprising user can find information on some of these work-study skills by extracting information from the first 34 items in the *Language* test and from 12 scattered items in the *Mathematics* and *Science* tests. The specialized skill of reading maps and charts can likewise be checked since it comprises the last 24 items in the *Social Studies* test. The lack of convenient norms on this combination of items and the size of the task of extracting information in such a fashion suggest that these portions of the reading act will be examined by few users of the battery.

Summary

Although some of the components necessary for complete evaluation of the Metropolitan Reading tests have not been published as of this review, it seems apparent that the tests are technically well constructed. For the user wanting to evaluate a limited portion of the act of reading or to perform an initial screening of pupils for special services, the *Reading* subtest of the *Total Reading Test* seems worthy of consideration. The user who wants to examine reading in a broader scope would do well to consider giving the complete Metropolitan Achievement Test Battery and arranging for computer analysis of the parts mentioned.

• Nelson-Denny Reading Test

Reviewed by Roger Farr
Indiana University

Name of Test	**Subtests**	**Publication Date**
Nelson-Denny Reading Test	*Vocabulary* *Comprehension* *Rate*	1929
Revision Date	**Authors**	**Publisher**
1960	M. J. Nelson E. C. Denny J. I. Brown	Houghton-Mifflin
Time		
40		

Overview

The Nelson-Denny Reading Test is designed for use in grades 9 through 16 and is available in two separate forms. The authors state that the test serves predictive, screening, and broadly diagnostic purposes. Three subtest scores are available: *Rate, Vocabulary,* and *Comprehension.* The *Vocabulary* test consists of one hundred multiple-choice items and is a timed (10 minutes) test; the *Comprehension* test, which is also timed (20 minutes), consists of 36 multiple-choice items based on a series of reading selections; the *Rate* score is based on the number of words of the first comprehension selection which an examinee reads during the first minute of the comprehension test.

Five kinds of answer sheets are available: IBM sheets (1230s and 805s) for machine or hand scoring, MRC answer cards for machine scoring, a self-marking answer sheet with a carbon marking system, and Digitek. The directions are clear and complete; however, examinees should be watched carefully when they move from the *Vocabulary* to the *Comprehension* tests as the test booklets must be turned over, the *Comprehension* subtest being printed on the back of the *Vocabulary* subtest.

The total test score is arrived at by allowing two points for each comprehension question that is answered correctly and one point for each vocabulary question answered correctly. The rationale for this procedure is that the total score will thus provide a better balance between the vocabulary and comprehension factors. Twice as much time, however, is allotted to the *Comprehension* test as to the *Vocabulary* test. The lack of any empirical basis for the scoring procedure is regrettable.

Norms

A stratified random sample of 8,472,478 subjects yielding 20,866 tested subjects was used to establish the test norms for grades 9-12. The stratification was based on geographical region (eight sections of the country) and on community size (four population ranges). The norming population for the college grades (13-16) was randomly selected from five different types of higher education institutions. For both the high school and college samples, the norming population is of satisfactory size and has been adequately selected and described. It would have been helpful, however, if additional descriptive information such as socioeconomic levels and intelligence test scores had also been supplied for the norming groups.

The test authors do not make any recommendations or suggestions regarding the development of local norms. This reviewer has often found that the most meaningful test interpretations can be made when a test score is compared to a population with which the test user is quite familiar. Test consumers should, therefore, seriously consider the development of local norms for the specific uses and the specific situations in which they want to use this test.

Reliability

The reliability data are quite insufficient. The sample sizes used are extremely small and inadequately described. Test consumers, therefore, should not rely on the reliability coefficients in the manual as a guide to interpreting test scores. The coefficients which are reported are of sufficient magnitude, but there is no way of knowing if the populations studied are comparable to the population an examiner is testing. In addition, the manual reports a reliability coefficient of .93 for the one minute rate test.

In a number of studies, however, this reviewer has been unable to establish a reliability coefficient for the rate measure even approaching .80.

The procedures used to develop the Standard Error of Measurement Table in the reliability section are not described. It could not be determined what population was used to compute the standard errors for the various subtests reported in the table. Under this condition little reliance should be placed in the data in this table.

Validity

The validity evidence for the three stated test purposes (prediction, screening, and diagnostic) is generally inadequate. There is only one small predictive study reported in the manual. This study is not adequately described, nor can much use be made of it for making predictive decisions about students.

The diagnostic validity evidence for the subtests is completely lacking. Not only do the test authors fail to report any evidence regarding the amount of overlap between subtests, the authors also seem to be unfamiliar with this usual state of affairs. In discussing uses of the test, the authors state: "More often than not, however, a student's test profile will show one area well above or below the others." Anyone who has spent much time studying the research on reading test validity will easily recognize the invalidity of this statement.

The development of the test does, however, seem to provide both face and content validity for using the test as a general screening measure for assessing students' reading abilities. In addition, the carefully developed norm sample and the percentile and grade norm tables provide a useful means for interpreting the scores.

Evaluation of Subtests and Items

The attempt to develop a reading test which spans eight grade levels is probably a mistake. A test which is difficult enough for college seniors will certainly have little bottom in it to measure the reading ability of the average ninth grade student. This is a major weakness of all the items and subtests on the test.

In addition, both the *Vocabulary* and *Comprehension* subtests are timed so strictly that very few examinees can complete the test. Difficulty is built into the test, therefore, by the use of time restrictions rather than by measuring increased reading ability. These two subtests should be properly titled "Speed of Reading Vocabulary" and "Speed of Reading Comprehension."

Generally, the content of the test seems to be better suited to the reading interests and abilities of college students than it does to those of high school students. The content of the reading comprehension selections also seems to favor those students with literary interests. There is little emphasis on scientific-type reading material.

Summary

The Nelson-Denny reading test should be used only for broad screening purposes when an examiner wishes to determine students' speeds of reading. The test is heavily timed and is more suited to college students than to high school students. There is almost no evidence to support use of the test as a diagnostic or predictive measure.

The reliability and validity evidence is completely inadequate for most purposes. While the norming population is adequate, most test consumers would be better off to develop local norms for their own situations. Despite the fact that the Nelson-Denny has been a favorite of teachers for many years, there are several other high school and college reading tests on the market which have sounder theoretical bases and which will serve most testing needs more adequately than the Nelson-Denny.

• The Nelson Reading Test

Reviewed by Lawrence M. Kasdon

Ferkauf Graduate School, New York City

Name of Test	**Subtests**	
Nelson Reading Test	*Vocabulary* *Comprehension*	
Revision Date	**Author**	**Publisher**
1962	M. J. Nelson	Houghton-Mifflin
Time		
40		

Overview

The Nelson Reading Test, Revised Edition, is a new edition published in 1962 and developed to replace the Nelson Silent Reading Test. The test has two forms, A and B. It is designed to measure vocabulary and comprehension for grades 3-9. The test yields three scores – vocabulary, paragraph comprehension, and total reading score. Examiner's Manual, Self-Marking Answer Sheets, IBM Answer Sheets, Digitek Answer Sheets, and Glass Record Sheets are available. For a fee, Houghton-Mifflin will score answer sheets and provide building and School System Percentile Norms.

In addition to the scoring methods indicated, the IBM scoring keys can be used for hand scoring answers recorded on IBM answer sheets. Tables are provided in the manual to convert subtest and total test raw scores to grade and percentile norms. These tables were standardized at midyear so that percentile scores for the beginning or end of the year are arrived at by interpolation. For example, if a sixth grade child's total reading raw score is 61 on a test administered in September, this score would place him at the 21st percentile according to the sixth grade norms and at the 47th percentile according to the fifth grade norms. The test author concluded, "Therefore, a reasonable expectation for this child would be a rank at the 34th percentile – halfway between the two percentile ranks determined previously."

The author is frank in mentioning the limitations of grade equivalent scores. Again, since the test was standardized in January, all other scores are obtained by interpolation. Although it is expensive to standardize a test, the author and the publishers ought to standardize a test at the beginning, middle, and end of the school year in order to offer the consumer viable norms.

The total score represents the total number of items correct. Separate sets of percentile and grade norms have been calculated for these raw scores.

The *Examiner's Manual* is reasonably satisfactory in format and content. All directions to be read to the pupils are printed in boldface type, and directions for the examiner are in regular type. Both types of directions are simple and clear-cut. The manual contains tables of percentile rank for each grade level as well as a grade equivalent norm table. Raw scores can be converted to these two statistics in a straightforward manner. The section "Some Uses of the Test" is probably the weakest part of the manual. After a brief discussion of how to use the test data, the author, to his credit, confesses that his suggestions for using the test results are superficial. His major problem is that he tries to use a survey test as if it were a diagnostic test.

Norms

The test was normed on approximately 18,000 students in 53 communities in 37 states. The author states that the samples were selected to represent four regions in the United States and that these areas were further stratified by community size. Although the author tried to obtain 30 percent of his samples from the Southern states, he, in fact, obtained 40 percent from this area of the country, leaving other areas underrepresented in the standardization. A list of communities was randomly selected within the size and regional strata. A responsible person in the school system of the community was asked to select classrooms at random. The appropriate level of the Henmon-Nelson Test of Mental Ability was administered to the standardization group. The mean IQs for the various levels ranged from 103.19 to 109.73 with the median at 106.46. In view of these findings, the author of the test reviewed 11 studies in which the Henmon-Nelson test was used. He found that the Henmon-Nelson generally yielded slightly lower means than other individual and group intelligence tests. He concluded that the Nelson Reading Test standardization sample was above average. By statistical procedures he brought the average IQ of the standardization sample to 100 for each grade level.

Within the limitations mentioned the norms can be cautiously accepted as being representative of national performance. The author does suggest the development of local norms, and this reviewer feels that local norms would make for a more precise and meaningful interpretation of the reading scores.

To obtain a minimum grade score of 2.00 on either *Vocabulary* or *Comprehension,* the student must have a raw score of seven items correct, an amount which seems empirically appealing. Again, this reviewer would like to point out that this test may not discriminate well among students in the third and fourth grades of less-than-average ability in reading. In as much as the test was standardized on samples from grades 3-9, grade scores below 3.5 and above 9.5 are interpolations and must be regarded with caution. The percentile ranks would not adequately reflect the performance of extreme groups since the tables do not reflect either a floor or ceiling effect.

Reliability

Reliability indexes were computed by the alternate-form procedure so that the consumer can judge how accurately a score on one form of the test will be reproduced if he measures students on another form of the test. Reliabilities are reported for *Vocabulary, Comprehension,* and *Total Score* at each grade level and for each of the two forms of the test. The author does not offer any information about the samples on which the reliabilities were computed except that they varied in size from 81 to 105 students. More information is necessary before one is able to interpret these reliabilities for his class. Also, the author does not state whether both forms of the test were administered on the same day, on alternate days, or a year apart. The alternate-form reliabilities for *Vocabulary* and *Comprehension* range from .81-.89 and for the *Total Score* from .88-.93. Alternate-form reliability is a rather conservative estimate of test reliability, and the figures reported are satisfactory.

Another type of information on the test's reliability is available in terms of the standard error of measurement for both raw scores and grade equivalents for each grade on both forms of the test. If a student were tested many times on a series of equivalent tests, disregarding such elements as practice and fatigue, his score would vary; the *standard error of measurement* is the calculated estimate of this variation.

Validity

The evidence of the validity of the test is rather limited. Except for the addition of two paragraphs to each form, all of the items by and large were selected from the three forms of the earlier edition of the test. Thus, most of the content is from the 1930s. Therefore, on whatever basis the content was selected in the 1930s and to the extent that the reading curriculum has changed since, the curricular validity of the test is weakened. Teachers are advised to examine this test to be sure that it adequately measures the objectives of their reading programs.

A case for the concurrent validity of the Nelson is made by citing correlations between it and the Iowa Test of Basic Skills. The *Vocabulary* and *Comprehension* subtests correlate from .62-.88. These correlations reflect moderate to high concurrent validity. The Nelson Reading Test together with the Nelson-Denny Reading Test are intended to provide continuous measurement of reading ability from Grade 3 through the adult level. The correlation between the two tests for 247 ninth graders was .82 for *Vocabulary,* .76 for paragraph *Comprehension,* and .84 for *Total.* One can conclude that both tests are measuring the same skills to a fair degree.

Nearly 92 percent of the students participating in the standardization were administered the appropriate level of the Henmon-Nelson Tests of Mental Ability as well as the Nelson Reading Test. One cannot help but wonder if the loss of 8 percent of the cases had a significant effect on the makeup of the original standardization group. Only correlations of total scores for both tests are given in the manual. For the establishment of concurrent validity the correlations are sufficiently large. Unfortunately, no information is given on the correlation between the *Verbal* subtest of the Henmon-Nelson and the Nelson Reading Test subtests as one would expect such correlation to be quite high. The correlations for these total scores do not reflect the usual pattern of growing larger as comparisons are made with higher grade levels. This point should warrant investigation.

Evaluation of Subtests

Both forms of the test contain 100 vocabulary items and 75 comprehension questions. The working time for the *Vocabulary* section is 10 minutes and for *Comprehension*, 20 minutes. Considering the number of items and the time limits, this is a combination of a speed test and a power test.

The *Vocabulary* test contains 100 words of increasing difficulty. The five multiple-choice answers are sometimes synonymous with the word tested; in other cases, they are descriptive of function or attribute, with an occasional antonym added for even greater variety. This variation requires considerable mental agility on the part of the pupil. On occasion, the word being tested is easier than the answer: "A quart is a measure of 1) enthusiasm 2) opportunity 3) capacity 4) temperature 5) geometry." This part of the test may be too difficult for third graders of less-than-average ability and may yield little information about them.

Paragraph *Comprehension* consists of 26 paragraphs of increasing difficulty. Except for a couple of the last paragraphs, the style and content smack of the contents of reading texts of the pre-Sputnik era. The information contained in Test Paragraph X, Form B, on interplanetary travel is somewhat dated. Each paragraph is followed by three multiple-choice questions. Each of the three questions is designed to measure a different type of comprehension – general meaning, details, and predicting outcomes. Having a predicting-outcome question for each paragraph means that the paragraphs had to be written for that purpose. For reasons known best to himself, the author has mixed the order of these three types of questions. This practice disregards the importance of setting purpose for reading and confuses the pupil who has established a set from working the sample paragraph. See Practice Exercise, question 1, for example. In other cases, some of the questions do not fit the categories the author has established. For example, see question 18, Form A.

Summary

The Nelson Reading Test provides a general measure of reading achievement for grades 3.5-9.5. From a statistical point of view the tests are well constructed. Unfortunately, little information is given about the samples on which reliability and validity data are based; thus, the user cannot know whether these data would apply to his population. The grade equivalent norms are somewhat restricted at the lower and upper ends of the test. If a teacher is satisfied using percentile ranks, those in the manual are quite adequate for grades 3.5-9.5. The words in the vocabulary section and the paragraphs used for comprehension appear to be somewhat dated. In addition, a few paragraphs contain inaccurate information, e.g., "tigers do not inhabit forests" (Test Paragraph 5, Form A).

The tests have been normed only for the midyear (January) so that interpolations, based on the rather untenable assumption that growth in reading throughout the year is uniform, need to be made to obtain percentiles for the beginning and end of the year. A teacher should carefully compare her objectives in reading with those of the test, when thinking about its validity. The interform reliability of the test is quite adequate. Perhaps the greatest advantages of the test are in its range of grades covered and that one can survey a small part of a group's reading abilities in only half an hour.

• Sequential Tests of Educational Progress, Series II: Reading

Reviewed by Thomas Estes,

University of Virginia

Name of Test	Subtests	Publication Date
STEP: Reading	None	1969
Author	**Publisher**	**Time**
Cooperative Tests and Services	Educational Testing Service	45 minutes

Overview

The new STEP Reading Test is part of STEP Series II, a comprehensive battery of tests designed to measure ability and achievement in reading and various subject areas of the curriculum with a view to improvement of instruction.

The test is available in two equivalent forms, A and B, and four levels, 1 through 4. It spans a grade range of possible use from grade 4 to grade 14. By contrast, its breadth of focus is more limited since the only score yielded is of *Reading Comprehension.* Vocabulary and speed subscores are not computed. The 65 items are split into two parts Part I, a 30-item, 15-minute vocabulary and sentence completion test, and Part II, a 35-item, 30-minute paragraph comprehension test. These combine to yield one score.

As a part of the STEP Battery or as a broad screening device for general reading skill, the test is useful. Those, however, who have in mind more diagnostic purposes or who desire a test which will yield reading subscores will have to look elsewhere.

Hand or machine scoring may be utilized with either of two standard IBM answer sheets, the 850 or the 1230. Use of the scoring service provided by ETS requires use of NCS answer sheets.

Directions for administration and scoring of the test appear to be clearly stated, though the directions may not emphasize strongly enough the importance of replicating as nearly as possible the exact conditions under which standardization took place. Raw scores transform easily to converted scores, percentile bands, percentile ranks, and stanines.

The STEP battery of tests shares a common weakness with its similar competitors: any specific test tends to be lost in the crowd, so to speak. Manuals and books of norms do not focus directly and clearly enough on the needs of a person using only one of the tests. Attempts to deal with the problem in this case seem to have resulted in a thick, finely printed book of norms and a scanty, rather non-specific user's manual. It seems strange that a test enjoying such wide acceptance and of such overall quality as this one provides so little user's assistance in its manuals. Hopefully, later editions of the manuals, along with a more comprehensive handbook, will remedy this problem.

Norms

The normative sample used for this test is not clearly defined by the preliminary handbook. The claim is for a representative sample of students at all educational levels, but procedures by which this representation was insured are not mentioned.

Whatever its exact nature, the sample on whom the reading was standardized was adequate in size for levels 2, 3, and 4 (grades 10-12, 7-9, and 4-6). The total number of pupils tested was 26,678. Unfortunately, for level 1, the college level test, a very small sample was drawn, numbering a scant 921.

While national norms have advantages, most meaningful interpretation of test results is often obtained by use of local norms. Cooperative Tests and Services provides a scoring service for users of the STEP which includes a computation of local norms as one reference group, in addition to the nationally drawn reference group. Users of the test should consider taking advantage of this valuable service.

Reliability

A reliability coefficient and a standard error of measurement are provided for every grade level in which the test should be administered. For Form A, 1,000 pupils were used to generate this data at each grade level. Perhaps as a reflection of this amount, the reliabilities for Form A are sufficient in magnitude and stability across grades, ranging from .88 to 92. For Form B, this is not the case: a much smaller population was used, and the reliabilities range from .84 to .95.

There is no mention of how the pupils were chosen for the reliability study. Worse still, no mention is made of the method used to derive the reliabilities. This is an important consideration for timed-reading tests; until more information may be made available, caution should be exercised regarding faith in the reported reliabilities.

Validity

The present manual of this test never directly addresses the question of validity. This omission is unfortunate in light of the claim that the test is designed principally as an aid in improvement of instruction. No evidence is offered to suggest that the test predicts reaction to improved instruction. There is no evidence, furthermore, that the results are in any way related to other measures, either in the STEP battery or apart from it, or that the manner in which reading is defined by the test is justifiable. Such criterion and construct-validity information is forthcoming in a promised technical manual, unavailable at the time of this review. Even so, the test is at best prematurely available for use; at worst, it is still in its experimental infancy, despite the tenure of the STEP battery.

The authors do, on the other hand, provide evidence of content validity. A separate table of specifications is given for each level of Form A. These allow the user to examine the kinds of comprehension the test claims to measure. More precisely, he can determine what each item in the comprehension section claims to measure. For example, in Form 3A, items 3, 12, and 26 of Part B intend to measure "straight-forward comprehension" of "science material"; item 23 and 27, on the other hand, assess "evaluation of logic" in "narrative" material. Used with the discretion the manual suggests, this information could be valuable.

In sum, this test's strongest suit is content validity. It appears to tap a range of reading abilities, broadly classed as vocabulary and comprehension. In the comprehension section readers deal with a variety of material types in a variety of ways. The test calls for at least six kinds of comprehension: "straightforward" comprehension, drawing inferences, understanding main ideas and supporting details, seeing applications, evaluating logic, and sensing style and tone. It is sadly unfortunate that the validity of such an instrument has to be taken at face value only – empirical evidence would inestimably increase its worth.

Evaluation of Items

The provision of four separate levels of this test is appropriate since the difficulty of the items is likely to be more in keeping with the abilities of the majority of pupils taking the test. In addition, the paragraphs on the test cover a range of possible interest value. The reading passages are appealing in both content and length, and questions are asked in a sensible, noninsulting fashion.

In format the test is also pleasing. Type size is adequately adjusted for different levels, and directions to the examinee are clearly stated. The mechanics of taking the test should interfere minimally with results.

Summary

The *STEP Reading Test* is probably most effectively used as a part of the STEP battery of tests. In this setting, it can reveal a student's relative standing in reading as compared to other areas of achievement. Separated from its companion tests, however, the test loses its main strength.

A single reading score is provided, though a screening device in reading should probably include some estimate of speed and vocabulary. Moreover, the reliability and validity information for the test is limited. No reading test approaches perfection, nor will one until test consumers raise their voices higher in demand of better quality. Even so, much more confidence in this test would be inspired by a little more supporting data. Later editions of materials to accompany the tests may well provide the needful inspiration.

• SRA Achievement Series (Multilevel Edition)

Reviewed by Nancy Roser
University of Texas at Austin

Name of Test	Subtests	Publication Date
SRA Achievement Series (Multilevel Edition)	*Comprehension* *Vocabulary*	1954

Revision Date	Authors	Publisher
1963	L. P. Thorpe D. W. Lefever R. A. Nashlund	Science Research Associates

Time
77

Overview

The 1963 revision of the SRA Achievement Series incorporates a reading battery which yields *Comprehension* and *Vocabulary* scores for grades 7 through 9, as well as a supplementary *Work-Study Skills* test. The publishers suggest that, while the revision is designed to provide a complete battery of scores in seven areas, any single subtest can be purchased and administered separately. The revised forms (C and D) reflect changes in educational content and sequence that have taken place since the earlier forms (A and B) were published in 1954-1957.

A unique feature of the total test, and consequently of the reading and study skills batteries, is that it is multilevel in nature; i.e., while the test is packaged as a whole for grades 4 through 9, the student's entry and stopping points vary with his grade placement and the time of year in which the test is administered. The content of the levels overlaps to provide continuity and to allow testing for a broad range of achievement within a group of students. Entry points are color coded with the students' answer sheets, green being the representative color for grade 7 and red for grade 9. The test administrator may elect either green or red during the student's eighth grade year, thus opting for a lower or higher level entry point depending upon prior testing and performance data collected. No specific criterion for making the appropriate entry point decision is provided; but suggestions are made as to grade levels at which the tests are most often administered, the grades and time of year for which norms are available, and the possible range of grade equivalent scores.

It would have been helpful if the test authors had provided more descriptive information pertaining to methods of item validation and placement. The consumer must make some assumptions that the test items are suitably scaled in difficulty so that different entry points are meaningful.

Student responses to either of the two forms are recorded on Docutran scoring sheets, which can be either hand-scored or returned to SRA for machine scoring. If SRA scores the response sheets, information is provided as to 1) list report of scores, 2) ranked list report of scores, 3) report of average scores, 4) special report of average scores, 5) local percentile norms and frequency distributions, 6) individual labels for cumulative records, 7) pupil progress and profile charts, 8) item analysis report, and 9) individual item reports.

In other words, SRA will provide such information as rank order, grade placement equivalents, stanines, and percentiles based upon raw score to allow group and individual comparisons through use of local norms, as well as information as to how the group being tested compares with a representative national sample. It seems valuable to note that the response sheet can be coded with other pertinent data about a particular student being tested, e.g., his sex, intelligence quotient, and/or some sociometric indicator so that group comparisons can be made during the inhouse scoring. In addition, teachers are supplied with individual pupil profiles indicative of each pupil's performance on each test item. The publishers make the latter information readily available to facilitate diagnostic planning and instruction.

Accessories for the test include: 1) an examiner's manual, 2) a general guide for planning and organizing the testing program, 3) an interpretive manual for groundwork in terminology and application, and 4) a technical manual for test technicians. The *Examiner's Manual* is thorough and complete. Parts which are to be read to the students are printed with a contrasting ink color and inset. An interpretive manual provides a basic and detailed guide to utilization of the test results as well as simple, yet cogent, definitions of terms. The test administrator is led to recognize the value of local norms and to realize that the benefits of a standardized instrument are contingent upon appropriate application and interpretation. The decision to publish separately the *Interpretive Guide* from the shorter accompanying booklet *Organizing Your Testing Program* appears to be an unfortunate one. The user may find himself shuffling booklets if he fails to keep separate the information contained in each. The technical manual has strengths in its clarity and thoroughness in reporting.

Time allotments are specific and generous. The total time for the reading test is 77 minutes, including directions. Time for the *Work-Study Skills* test is 76 minutes, including directions. Because a power test (rather than a speeded test) was the authors' intent, approximately 90 percent of the students are expected to finish within the required time.

Norms

The standardization sample for the total test consisted of 71,199 subjects in grades 1 through 9. Obtaining a proportionate geographical representation, while giving attention to urban versus rural residence, was the one criterion in selection of the sample for each grade level. The manual, however, provides no information specific to the manner in which the sample was drawn. What the user can determine from the technical manual is that in order to arrive at proportional representations from each geographical category, an undetermined number of students were randomly eliminated from overrepresented areas and randomly duplicated in underrepresented areas. In all, over 20 percent of the standardization sample was excluded in determining the norms.

Reliability

Reliability coefficients are provided for all subtests of both forms. Coefficients appear sufficiently high across all batteries, with composite reliabilities on the multilevel edition equal to or greater than .97. Only the Kuder-Richardson Formula 20 was used to compute reliability. While this is one suitable attempt to estimate one source of variance, other reliability measures could have been employed to examine other sources of variance.

Validity

The authors suggest that the test be examined by each administrator for content validity, i.e., each user should compare the content and skills of his curricular intent with the test itself. After building a case for the value of overlapping content, the authors defend the face validity of the test, adhering to the belief that such measures can provide for continuity of evaluation in a seamless curriculum.

In order to derive some validity estimates, an attempt was made to determine the number of independent dimensions measured by the series. The subtests were analyzed by use of the principal-components method of factor analysis. The factor loadings resulting from the analysis included: 1) thoughtful reading, 2) computational (quantitative) ability, and 3) language ability. The data indicated consistency across level and form in the *Achievement* series as well as indicating that different broad abilities were being measured by the *Language Arts, Arithmetic,* and *Reading* batteries.

Finally, an attempt was made to estimate the validity of the Multilevel Edition by examining the correlation between grade equivalent scores taken one year apart on different forms. The median correlation between subtest forms was .76, with a range from .62 to .88 for the series. Correlations for *Reading Comprehension* and *Reading Vocabulary* were .72 and .69, respectively, between Forms C and D.

Evaluation and Subtests

The format of the total test is such that story materials are drawn from the fields of social studies, science, and literature. The relatively lengthy selections are followed by items purporting to assess the students' abilities to understand the overall theme, to identify the main ideas in paragraphs, to infer logical results, to retain significant details, and, finally, to understand the meaning of words in context (the latter score constituting the *Vocabulary* subtest score). At the upper levels, approximately four questions are devoted to literary interpretation of two poems. The authors believe that the ability to retain ideas in order to make comparisons, as well as the ability to read at a reasonable rate, is assessed incidentally.

Vocabulary words are underlined in the context of each passage. Students are asked to select the appropriate meaning or shade of meaning from one to four choices. By presenting vocabulary words in context, the authors have avoided one common criticism levied against many reading tests. Three word lists were consulted to check the appropriateness of subtest vocabulary (Gates, Rinsland, and Thorndike, Lorge). The user might be justified in questioning the validity of these lists in view of the ages of the instruments as well as the differing data collection techniques employed by each compiler.

The *Work-Study Skills* subtest (published separately) yields scores on *References* and *Charts.* The *References* subtest yields a measure of competence in the use of the table of contents, index, and general reference material. The *Charts* score is based upon achievement in interpreting charts, graphs, maps, and tables. Representative selections from elementary and junior high textbooks, newspapers, and magazines were included. The most heavily assessed skill in the *Reference* subtest is the ability to select an appropriate encyclopedia volume while interpretation of bar and circle graphs receive most attention in the *Charts* subtest.

Summary

The SRA Achievement Series (Reading) appears to have several strengths to recommend its use, including ease of administration, clarity of format, and continuous, overlapping tests which allow closer approximations of the extremes within a classroom. The large standardization sample, as well as the provision for local norms facilitating inter- and intragroup comparison, contributes to the value of the instrument.

The time limit is reasonable, although longer than the average class period. The three reading scores (*Vocabulary, Comprehension*, and *Total Reading*) seem to be a logical breakdown.

Editor's note: Two new forms of the *SRA Achievement Series* (E and F) are currently being standardized, too late for inclusion in this review. Full scoring service for the new forms will be available in Fall 1971, with complete technical information available in January 1972.

• Stanford Achievement Test: High School Reading

Reviewed by J. Jaap Tuinman

Indiana University

Name of Test	**Subtests**	**Publication Date**
Stanford Achievement Test: High School Reading	None	1922
Revision Date	**Authors**	**Publisher**
1965	E. F. Gardner J. C. Merwin R. Callis R. Madden	Harcourt Brace Jovanovich

Overview

This test is one of a ten-test battery of achievement tests for use in grades 9-12. As such it is an upward extension of the Stanford Achievement Test, grades 1-9, which has been on the market since 1922, with the latest edition published in 1964.

The *Reading* Test has three forms: W, X, and S. Only the first two are available for normal use. The latter form is a so-called "secure" form, to be used only in special testing programs under conditions which warrant minimal exposure of its content to unqualified persons (such as students who have to take the test at some later time).

According to the publisher's promotional flyer this test is "a measure of paragraph comprehension, testing ability to understand what is explicit in the material read, to judge what is implied, and to draw inferences applicable to other situations." The manual accompanying the reading test gives little additional information about the purpose of the test: "The *Reading* test consists of paragraphs of increasing length from a half-dozen lines to paragraphs of nearly 40 lines. Multiple-choice questions are used to measure the comprehension of the paragraph." In all there are 65 questions. In addition to the paragraphs with multiple-choice questions, there are paragraphs in which words have been deleted. Comprehension of those paragraphs is measured by having the student select the best word to fill the blank from four choices. (The publisher should note that at least one story exceeds the 40 lines mentioned in the foregoing quote.)

The test results in a single raw score; there are no subtests. The directions for administration are very clear. The test itself requires 40 minutes; in addition, about 10 minutes are needed for distributing materials, completing the identifying information section, and giving general directions. Four different types of answer sheets are available for use with the test: IBM 805, IBM 1230, Digitek, and MRC. Appropriate directions for administering each type are provided in the answer sheet packages. The test can be hand scored using an overlay key. Users must keep in mind that students marking more than one option for an answer may have an advantage unless the answer sheets are checked for such practice. Complete scoring and reporting service is available from the publisher for MRC, IBM 805, and IBM 1230 answer sheets. Two types of class records are available – one for use with the 12 tests in the complete battery of the Stanford High School Test and an abridged version with space for eight tests designed to be used with individual tests or in combination thereof.

The manual is in general a prime example of what an up-to-date test manual should be. The variety of information which the manual contains and the care with which premises and implications have been stated are exemplary. The development of the test is described in satisfactory detail, although the description of the tryout program is rather elaborate. Among the other attractive features of the manual are its well-balanced discussion of the use of the test results and the judicious inclusion of relevant and clear tabular material. Unfortunately, no special manual for the separate tests seems to be available. As a consequence, specific suggestions regarding the use of scores of one particular test, such as *Reading,* are scarce.

Norms

The standardization program is described adequately. The final norms are based on a sample of 22,699 students spread rather evenly over the four grades (9-12). Participating schools were selected from nine geographic regions, including all 50 states. An attempt was made to insure proper socioeconomic representation; however, the manual is a little unclear in regard to this issue. Norms are expressed in terms of a standard score with a mean of 50 and a standard deviation of 10 percentiles and stanines. The meaning of each of these statistics is discussed in clear language. For *Reading,* three norm-groups are provided: the total standardization group by grade; the subset of students from the total group who expressed intent to pursue college work; and a so-called ability group where "ability" is defined in terms of stanine score on the Otis Quick Scoring Mental Ability Test: Gamma Test. The approach taken by the authors allows a very extensive interpretation of a student's score. Yet, there are a few questions. The manual points out that the norms are based on performance at the beginning of the second semester. If a user tests at a much earlier or much later time, it is suggested that adjustments should be made. While the suggestion is correct, it seems meaningless in terms of the course of action an individual user can take. How is he going to "adjust"? Also, using the Otis Test as a measure of "ability" is questionable. Scores on this test are for the most part as much a function of "achievement" as are the reading scores themselves. This fact becomes evident from the systematic increase of mean scores with increase in grade (Table 3, p. 12). In this respect it is also relevant that if one estimates the reliability of the

Otis at .90, the correlation between *Reading* and IQ, corrected for unreliability in both tests, becomes virtually perfect.

In general, however, the norms and the suggestions for their use are well developed, well presented, and most useful.

Reliability

The reliability data reported are as complete as any user would desire. All coefficients exceed .90. In addition, the standard error of measurement is given in terms of T-scores, and its use is discussed. This is a most desirable feature. The fact that the standard errors are reported only for the combined grades is of little importance since neither standard deviation nor reliabilities vary much across grades. The standard error given, therefore, is safe for use in all grades.

Validity

According to the authors of the various kinds of validity discussed, content validity is "the most important and directly relevant" (P. 15). This reviewer agrees. It is, therefore, disappointing that after a very good definition of content validity, the only evidence presented consists of a table which classifies the items by the nature of the *materials* from which the passages have been drawn. No information is given regarding the "behavior," or, as the manual puts it, the "skills, knowledges, and understandings" tapped by the test. As is the case with many other reading tests, the easy way out has been chosen by practically redefining "content validity" in terms of curricular materials only. An analysis of the tests themselves reveals the narrow scope of what the test measures. First of all, "reading" is equated with paragraph comprehension. "Paragraph comprehension" is defined in terms of filling in missing words and answering multiple-choice questions. The *content* validity of the first task is obscure though its correlation with question-type tasks is well established. The content validity of the question-type tasks depends on the nature of their questions. Test writers should present some kind of analysis of their questions in an attempt to facilitate the user's judgment of the validity of the test for their own purposes. It appears to this reviewer that the items in this test are the usual mixture of questions involving various cognitive levels of operation with a preponderance of items at the level of literal understanding.

In regard to the issue of content validity and equivalence of forms, it may be noted that the X and W forms differ considerably in regard to the type of tasks included. Form W has nine short passages with 23 words left out in all, i.e., 23 fill-in items; Form X has eight such stories with 29 fill-in items. Form W has six longer passages with 42 questions whereas Form X has five such passages with 36 questions. While the test forms were statistically equated, assurance of equal content validity cannot be given.

No criterion-related-validity evidence is presented other than correlations with the other nine tests in the battery. In general, these correlations are high. Their meaning and the meaning of the resulting factor analysis cannot be adequately determined without additional data not normally part of the evidence reported in a test manual.

In regard to the validity issue it may be mentioned that the publisher offers to make available to the users a continuously updated bibliography of materials related to the use of the test. The copy of this bibliography received by this reviewer upon his request, however, was compiled in 1966.

Summary

Within the limits of its validity, the Stanford Achievement Test – *High School Battery: Reading* is a good test. Its manual in particular is excellent. It can be recommended without hesitation for those users who have measurement needs covered by this test; that is, those users for whom the test has validity.

No technical excellence can void the fact that as a test of reading this test has a narrow scope. This scope can be best described as the largely literal understanding of short paragraphs of rather simple structure and filled with factual details. For those users who feel that the type questions and tasks used in this test are those they would employ to measure reading, this test should be a serious candidate. Those users who want a more extensive and more complete inventory of a student's reading ability should not consider it.

• Traxler High School Reading Test – Revised

Reviewed by J. Jaap Tuinman

Indiana University

Name of Test	Subtests	Publication Date
Traxler High School Reading Test – Revised	*Story Comprehension* *Word Meaning* *Paragraph Comprehension*	1938
Revision Date	**Author**	**Publisher**
1967	A. E. Traxler	Bobbs-Merrill

Overview

The Traxler High School Reading Test – Revised, an upward extension of the Traxler Silent Reading Test, is a revision of a test originally published in 1938. The test booklets for both forms (A,B), which have 1966 as a copyright date, carry the designation "for grades 10, 11, and 12." The *Manual of Directions,* which sets the date of revision at 1967, indicates that the test is intended for grades 9, 10, 11, and 12. In addition, norms for Grade 9 are provided. This discrepancy between manual and test booklets may cause some confusion.

The test was constructed to measure 1) rate of continuous reading of material in the social and natural sciences, 2) comprehension of that material at the rate read, and 3) understanding of main ideas presented in paragraphs taken from high school texts in social studies and science. The test does not contain a vocabulary section. Instead, the author recommends a separate 15-minute vocabulary test.

The 1967 revision does not differ much from the earlier version. The basic impetus for revision was the update of some obsolete items. The first part of both forms was virtually left unchanged. In the second part of Form A revisions were made in eight items whereas in Form B four items were updated.

The directions for administering and scoring the test are clear. The test takes 45 minutes in all. The time limits are very generous; most students will finish before time is called. The test can be either hand scored or machine scored. No test-specific answer sheets are provided, a condition which may be considered a plus point from an economic point of view.

In all, five scores are obtained: rate (1), story comprehension (2), main ideas (3), total comprehension (2 +3), and total score (1+2+3). The latter score is a little difficult to interpret: Why would one want to add rate (as defined in this test) and the comprehension scores? Fortunately, the author is rather hesitant in his recommendations about the use of this total reading score. This reviewer advises never to use it. Not only is this score rather meaningless as a concept, but even in a technical sense it has little to recommend it. The mean scores for form B on the 1967 revision were as follows: rate, 35; story comprehension, 10; and main ideas, 19. These data mean that roughly 55 percent of the total score is accounted for by the rate component. These data also throw some light upon another setback of the rate score as it is defined in this test (unrelated to the comprehension score). An average student who does not read the passage at all can easily earn a total score of 62+5+19=86, which is far more than he would have obtained by conscientiously reading the story. (This hypothetical student is assigned the mean score for main ideas, 19.) Obviously, he must be smart enough to circle a word in the last line when time is called. Naturally, a set of scores as earned by this student should alert the user of the test. Such a student should be scheduled for special diagnostic attention. The high *total* score, however, may work as a deterrent in the case of casual usage of the test.

Norms

The norms for the Traxler High School Reading Test were obtained from a sample of 7,000 students from schools in the Eastern, Midwestern, Western, and Southern sections of the United States. The norming data were gathered for the 1938 edition. In the twelfth grade 1,164 students were included (the minimum) whereas 2,894 tenth graders were tested (the maximum). The description of norming population must be judged inadequate. Relevant information, e.g., socioeconomic criteria, is missing. No new norms were obtained for the revised edition. The author tried to determine whether such new norms were necessary. In the presentation of relevant data, information on the comparability of the revised B Form and the unrevised B Form is missing. With characteristic frankness the author concludes that the norms for the *Story Comprehension* may have to be somewhat adjusted. It is not clear how this could be done, however.

Reliability

The reliabilities reported for the subtests presumably are all corrected split-half correlations; the coefficient for the total test is based on the correlation between the two forms. All coefficients are based on extremely small groups of students (around 75). Comparison of the coefficients is

made difficult by the fact that different grades were used to obtain the various subtest reliabilities. The reliabilities are estimated as follows: rate, .90; story comprehension, .72; main idea, .80; total comprehension, .86; and total reading, .91. The author is careful to point out that with the exception of rate, the reliabilities of the subtests are too low to allow the tests to be used for individual assessment. His suggestion, though, that the "total score on the test is satisfactory for use in predicting the reading achievement of individual pupil" seems not to coincide with the caution he urged elsewhere in the manual in regard to the use of this total score.

Validity

No data on the validity of the test as such have been presented in the manual. The choice of passages may indicate that content validity in regard to the materials aspect of curriculum content in social studies and science may be assured. The same cannot be said of the behavior aspect of content validity, however. The questions in both sections seem to favor the lower cognitive skills.

Whereas data on content validity, criterion-related validity, and construct validity are absent, the manual does contain a section on "item validity." The data presented indicate that the average item in the tests does effectively discriminate between subjects who scored low and those who scored high on the total test. While the use of the term "validity" in this context is common, it is also slightly misleading. No conclusions about the validity of the test itself should be drawn from the information in this section.

Evaluation of Subtests

Part I of the Traxler High School Reading Test contains a story accompanied by 20 questions. When opening the booklet, the student first sees the questions, printed upside down, and the opening lines of the story. He is asked to read the story first and to circle the word he was reading when the examiner says "mark"; this sign is given at 150 and 300 seconds. The rate of reading is based on the position of the word marked. After completion of the story, the student turns back to the 20 questions. Though the instructions say "Read as fast as you can read *understandingly,* but no faster, as *you cannot work the exercises unless you know what you have read,*" there is some reason to believe that a larger-than-chance part of these questions can be answered without reading the story at all. Part of the reason may be that a large number of questions are based on only one selection of continuous prose. The number of questions answered right constitutes the *Story Comprehension* score, one of the two components of the *Total Comprehension* score.

Part II consists of thirty social studies and science paragraphs, each accompanied by four statements. The student's task is to identify the statement which contains the main idea of the paragraph. In general, each of the statements after the paragraph represents a minor paraphrase of a sentence in the paragraph. Once the student has determined which of the sentences in the paragraph itself is most important, his task is easy. No inferences involving relations among sentences are called for. It is doubtful that reading the passage is necessary for determining the main ideas. In many instances the right answer can be found without reading the passages at all. (For what it is worth, this reviewer's sophomore assistant obtained scores of 83 percent and 80 percent of the items right when attempting these items without being able to see the passages.)

Summary

Many of the criticisms herein can be leveled against almost any reading test currently on the market. Even so, the limited purpose of the test and its narrow definition of reading comprehension, in addition to the shortcomings mentioned, make this instrument unsuitable for general use as a survey test of reading. The rate section can well be used if the user finds a way of controlling deception on the part of an occasional student. Asking easier questions which, however, should be unanswerable without reading the passage may offer a possible solution for this problem. The selection of the passages seems to make the test of interest to the teacher in social studies and science. The potential user, however, will have to determine for himself whether he can live with the type of questions asked as a measure of comprehension of materials in these subject areas.

• The Traxler Silent Reading Test

Reviewed by Joseph P. McKelpin
Southern Association of Colleges and Schools

Name of Test	**Subtests**	**Publication Date**
Traxler Silent Reading Test	*Reading Rate* *Story Comprehension* *Word Meaning* *Paragraph Comprehension*	1934
Revision Date	**Author**	**Publisher**
1942	A. E. Traxler	Bobbs-Merrill
Time		
46 or 53		

Overview

The Traxler Silent Reading Test was designed to measure four aspects of reading ability for students in grades 7 through 10: rate, story comprehension, vocabulary, and paragraph comprehension. Forms 1 and 2 were first made available in 1934. Forms 3 and 4 were added in 1939 and 1942, respectively. The Traxler Reading Test has four subtests: *Reading Rate, Story Comprehension, Word Meaning,* and *Paragraph Comprehension.* When Forms 1 and 2 were first made available, Part III (*Paragraph Comprehension*) consisted of six paragraphs with three or four completion-type questions for each paragraph. According to the publisher's manual, a small study was carried out in 1968 in order to change the completion questions in the *Paragraph Comprehension* part of Forms 1 and 2 to multiple-choice items so that machine scoring could be used, if desired, with all parts of all forms of the test. The *Paragraph Comprehension* part of Forms 3 and 4 was machine scorable when those forms were first made available.

Examinee performance time is 46 minutes for the hand-scoring administration; for the machine-scoring administration, the examinee performance time is 53 minutes. Only on the test booklet for Form 1, Revised, do the directions include instructions to the student for use of a separate answer sheet. Since the directions on the other forms fail to include instructions for using a separate answer sheet for machine-scoring, the overall time requirements for administration may be greater for forms other than Form 1, Revised.

Norms

The publisher's manual indicates that norms were derived from about 25,000 pupils in grades 7, 8, 9, and 10. Apparently, results from grades 9 and 10 of the Michigan statewide testing program in 1937 and 1938 were combined with other available scores from schools elsewhere in the United States. The norms for Part III, *Paragraph Comprehension,* were adjusted in the 1969 revision on the basis of data collected for that edition.

Reliability

Equivalent forms reliability estimates are reported in the manual. They range from .613 for *Story Comprehension* to .950 for *Total Score.* The single comprehension estimates are the lowest ones in the set although estimates of combined and total comprehension seem highly reliable. For survey purposes, consequently, the test may be useful, but for diagnostic use with individual students it may be questionable.

Validity

Examination of the procedures and results of validity studies of the test indicates that it probably measures those aspects of reading ability selected. Still some questions do arise. The heavy weighting assigned to *Reading Rate* could result in yielding a total score out of proportion with the student's comprehension of what was read. The Inglis Test of English Vocabulary used as a criterion for word meaning may not have equal efficacy in all population groups. The use of 54 sixth grade students' composite scores to establish the validity of the comprehension tests for beginning seventh graders seems to stretch the permissible limits.

Evaluation of Subtests

The *Reading Rate* subtest requires the student to read material about animals as fast as is consistent with his being able to answer questions about the story later. In taking the subtest, the student is twice required to indicate the place he has reached in the reading – once at the beginning of 100 seconds and again at the end of 200 seconds. Numbers in the right margin opposite each line of the story are used to translate amount read into rate.

The *Story Comprehension* subtest measures the student's understanding of the story read in the *Rate* subtest. The student is to complete each of 10 sentences by selecting one of five options. This subtest is to be taken immediately upon completing the *Rate* test.

The *Word Meaning* subtest is a measure of vocabulary. The vocabulary words (underlined) are used in short sentences or phrases which are followed by five words or phrases. The student is to select the word or phrase whose meaning is most nearly like the meaning of the word underlined.

The *Paragraph Comprehension* subtest is designed to measure the ability to read material at varying levels of difficulty. The subtest consists of six paragraphs and 20 multiple-choice questions. The student is to read each paragraph and indicate his option for each of the three or four questions following it.

Summary

The Traxler Silent Reading Test seems to be a useful survey instrument to be employed with students in grades 7-10. The social class bias of some parts of the test, especially the *Word Meaning,* may reduce its efficacy for students from the lower social classes.

APPENDIX

The table of tests on the following pages provides quick reference to the basic information on each test reviewed in this book. The index provides a quick reference to the critiques of reading tests appearing in Buros' *Reading Tests and Reviews* (Highland Park, New Jersey: Gryphon Press, 1968) and to Buros' *Mental Measurement Yearbook* (Highland Park, New Jersey: Gryphon Press, 1938, 1940, 1949, 1953, 1959, 1965). These excellent test reviews should be studied before a test consumer makes a final test selection.

Within the table, tests are arranged alphabetically by name. The first six columns are self-explanatory. The next two columns are the index. In the first column of the index, the number to the left of the colon refers to the volume number of the *Mental Measurement Yearbook* in which the review appears; the numbers on the right of the colon refer to the review number in that volume. The numbers in the second column of the index refer to the page number in *Reading Tests and Review* on which the test is described and/or reviewed.

It should be noted that the reviews in *Reading Test and Reviews* are the same ones which have appeared in the *MMYs.* Both are listed here because a test consumer may have access to only one of these references.

Table of tests plus an index to READING TESTS AND REVIEWS and MENTAL MEASUREMENT YEARBOOKS

Test	Subtests	Latest Publication Date	Authors	Publisher	Time (min)	Volume and Test Number in Mental Measurement Yearbooks	Page in Reading Tests and Reviews
California Achievement Test: Reading	*Vocabulary* *Reading Comprehension*	1970	E. W. Tiegs W. W. Clark	Calif. Test Bureau/ McGraw-Hill	50	6:784	290
Cooperative English Tests Reading Sec.	*Vocabulary* *Comprehension*	1960	C. Derrick D. P. Harris B. Walker	Educational Testing Service	40	6:806	321
Davis Reading Test	*Level of Comprehension;* *Speed of Comprehension*	1961	F. B. Davis C. C. Davis	Psychological Corp.	40	6:786	291
Diagnostic Reading Tests	*Survey Section* *Diagnostic Battery*	1963	Committee on Diagnostic Reading Tests	Committee on Diagnostic Reading Tests	Varies	6:823	342
Gates-MacGinitie Reading Tests	*Vocabulary* *Comprehension*	1965	A. I. Gates W. MacGinitie	Teachers College Press, Columbia University	65	6:792	301
Iowa Silent Reading Tests	*Vocabulary* *Comprehension* *Directed Reading* *Reading Efficiency*	1973	H. A. Green V. H. Kelley	Harcourt Brace Jovanovich	60	6:794	307

Metropolitan Achievement Tests: Reading Advanced Level	*Word Knowledge* *Reading*	1970	W. W. Durost H. H. Bixler J. W. Wrightstone G. A. Prescott I. H. Balow	Harcourt Brace Jovanovich	Varies	6:797	311
Nelson-Denny Reading Test	*Vocabulary* *Comprehension Rate*	1960	M. J. Nelson E. C. Denny J. I. Brown	Houghton Mifflin	40	6:800	315
Nelson Reading Test	*Vocabulary* *Comprehension*	1962	M. J. Nelson	Houghton Mifflin	40	6:802	320
Sequential Tests of Educational Progress — Series II Reading	None	1969	Cooperative Tests and Services	Educational Testing Service	45		
SRA Achievement Series (Multilevel Edition)	*Comprehension* *Vocabulary*	1963	L. P. Thorpe D. W. Lefever R. A. Naslund	Science Research Associates	77	6:808	324
Stanford Achievement Test: High School Reading	None	1965	E. F. Gardner J. C. Merwin R. Callis R. Madden	Harcourt Brace Jovanovich	Varies	—	7
Traxler High School Reading Test — Revised	*Story Comprehension* *Word Meaning* *Paragraph Comprehension*	1967	A. E. Traxler	Bobbs-Merrill	55	4:559	187
Traxler Silent Reading Test	*Reading Rate* *Story Comprehension* *Word Meaning* *Paragraph Comprehension*	1942	A. E. Traxler	Bobbs-Merrill	55	4:560	187

international
book year
1972

UNESCO